TIME'S HAUNTED GENERATION

(BIG BANG NUTSHELL) TIME'S HAUNTED GENERATION

M. D. VERITAS

Bon Ton Republic Publications * New Orleans 2019

LUX ET VERITAS

To the memory of Susan Austell, Guy Charleville,
Maxine Cassin & Henry Ross

For Janice Charleville, Diana Boylston & Lin Emery

Behold, Thou desirest truth in the inward parts:
and in the secret part Thou shall make me to know wisdom.

To the chief musician: A Psalm of David (51:6)

Cover: Iconcurchaic Angel with Lin Emery's *Flight*
   (Icon + current + archaic = Iconcurchaic)

Numbers by titles in ( ) are Shakespeare Sonnets for allusions in *italics*

(Big Bang Nutshell) Time's Haunted Generation

Appendix

Acknowledgments
Grateful acknowledgment is made to the following publications where poems listed first appeared in different versions and titles:
Portals Press; Maple Leaf Rag Anthologies:
Resurrection Epiphany (Resurrection Visitation)
Yeats' Last Paradigm Vision (Adam's Blessing)
Her Unburdened Prescience (Maxine's Review)

Big Bang Nutshell Time's Haunted Generation

Visionary Angelic Visitation, 2011

One night in bed, lit window shade edge, framed seeping

sleep, stirred in shadows where feet were at foot of bed,

slow seated moves in hung clothes, draped chair, turning head,

a moment's dozed dream transfixed, angelic being.

My awe saw closer hooded face grow brighter

into her spectral beauty's up lifted bliss face,

brightening full moonlight, looked down, turned cloaked writer,

right-reached hand grasp-moved my left wrist to my chest space,

to bless will's written gesture, gracing checked terror

then vanished as I lurched full-eyed, grasp-moved, split fear

to circumnavigate a startled challenged heart.

Night's agon fought unknown what part of dream took part,

a face of greatest beauty shone immortal moon,

from greeting's peak joy to all's well seen, see you soon.

Blinded Sight to See

How does one move passed the past to transform, perchance

dream jeremiad elixir's new inwardness,

refused heresy's individual distance,

view dualist fallen state's redemption transcendence?

How blindness gives insight to sharpen soul senses

like Paul's Damascus fall encountered spirit's call,

where Milton's inner world cost his lost defenses

now makes of fallen paradigm's total recall

translated metamorphosis from faith's display

of unplanned blinding light on dark illumined braille,

feels floating steps off a precipice, walks away

through air-clocked safety nets till repercussions fail,

determined by inner light's counter ego,

perspective beats on eardrum's visionary flow.

Resurrection Epiphany

(149)

He left *me* waking to his death *defect* as prized,

a *call* then came from *half-forgotten* brother Dan

who said his father, *my despised* step-dad had died

then Dan disclosed Dad's *present* executor plan.

As if *commanded motion* made *my spent* dream

as I had *spied* three months back, soldier Dad,

in his resurrected body's *worship* gleam,

the vigor of Dad's infinite *loved* youth, undead.

Surpassing William Blake's sublime *mind*, his youth,

a love supreme, no *blind* sense's fearsome wrath

to greet me from old noble brownstone's *tyrant* truth,

partaking Jerusalem light's bright amber bath.

I let Dan know of dreadful *cruel* dreams before

Dad's *service merit*, cremated army honor.

No longer need I *see love* through a family chore

in crisp green fatigues *respected* from some deeds door.

In crisp green fatigues respected from some *deeds* door,

an army wooden white board hospital *skilled* wing,

he walked across a ramp's *warrant* transitioning

with quick *exceeding* steps to a brownstone porch floor.

He turned facing *my abhorrence* straight down the stairs,

his lingered smile, perfect *bright* recognition face

then let *me* feel the washed out *hate* displace

his sins in life, purged *worthiness* with *my* fears,

beside his serious *raised* gaze in awe at sky.

His breathless *heart* for this *powered* transition through

new life, allowed to lead *me taught* as I'd try

to view a *state* that happens, what leads to

the next phase *loving* brings after we die,

day's grace my eyes were meant to *see anew.*

(151)

Day's grace *my* eyes were meant to see anew,

he shared as *pointed out*, I followed *by his side*,

unsaid words, *wants* were felt, from sidewalks we arrived.

A building like the other *rose* up, looked into,

a few *young* men near touched up *gentle* plaster walls,

one kind resembled *me* in youth, through I moved

in part then walked *out*, though filled with gratitude,

not ready for *proud proof* beyond the halls & *calls*

or *noble* rooms they lead to, what they lit to see.

All races, city dressed *young* men & women

then walked about the streets *contented beside me.*

When I drew up to Dad's *love* as if unseen,

we *stood* at the next stone porch silently.

He stepped grand *rising* steps & through the door was gone.

Content internal radiance like fire baptized,

he left *me* waking to *his* death defect as *prized.*

In cold grey lit suburban tree-lined *misused* dream,

long shadowed driveway *bearing* sidewalks sloped away

from journey's *new eyes* to find young Mother's *faith* stream,

forsworn door opens, as *blind* slow walks a lady.

From shadowy exit *hated* trepidation,

a conscience of *perjured* insubordination,

gazed at *love's lie* to disarm abrogation

or dare collude with silence, *swear* life's negation.

As she approached wrapped in *constancy's* shroud,

got close, aimed several rifles, *accused* what I feared,

to *swear* this many times death she could have allowed,

my cringe *broke* her barrels, like my arm, disappeared.

She lifts a cowboy pistol to her *swearing* side,

pressed there with *vowed* face of self-annihilation,

appalled I stoop, stuck on the spot's *oath twice* denied,

reached out to shout, "Don't shoot!" *deep vowed* consternation

at bright shroud, pearl handle, fainting whites of her *eyes*,

no shot, *enlightened* fall's original surmise.

Truth reaffirms change, psyche's regeneration

unmasks fear-*torn* trial's haunted generation.

Monumental Proposal (*Lincoln/King*)   (66)

Two men, extreme roads apart, *rest* together,

took paths less traveled to *honored* martyrdom.

A century divides their death *desert* weather,

same destination, same *forsworn* sung kingdom.

Their ends could have come from the same *shameful* bullet,

in different centuries for the same *gilded* tomb,

looked to the same love's trusted *virtue*, desperate

room, *rightly* constituted civil future's home.

Opposing roads gathered to the same *disgraced* ends,

a war for peace, peace as a war of *tongue-tied* words,

conceived in liberty, mountaintop *doctor* friends

belong to the same shrine, hands on same *skilled* rewards.

The first, white marble perched *truth's simple* judgment seat,

the bronze one, *captain* tall, hand on first, complete.

Recycling Lee Circle (67)

In dream Lee's column *presence* stood down recycled,

film panned up column, *achieved* Lin Emery's "Flight,"

replaced Lee, north defiant, *impious*, shackled

back to his wealth of *nature*, Arlington's grave site.

His door to war's *poor* bled garden of dry bones,

so many dead occupy Lee's *advantaged* house,

where column *shadows indirectly seek* headstones

as he lies low, overseeing *roses*, live moss,

defined in statuettes, lost *imitates* what's found,

arms folded defied sky, still *proud* automaton,

as Dixie plays, celebrates the *exchequer* pound,

entombed *grace* best saved, New Orleans, Lafayette One.

To rest the Mason-Dixon's lined up *bankrupt* friend,

George Washington's words *gained* then rang in the wind:

"We either are to *live* with slaves," he *living* wrote,

"or happy plains drenched in *blood*," Lee would *paint* the quote.

Last monuments *so bad, infection spread to boss,*

though Jackson won, *society* made Lee's *sin* loss.

10

As Ai Weiwei contemplates art's *second* weight,

consuming fate to stay in the Chinese state,

two soldiers stand by his sleep deprived *dead-bed* cell,

make sure no dreams get *nourished* for his pen to tell,

no chairs made from *expired* police batons,

unsealed case bottoms for concealed "Fake Carry-ons."

Before his lawyer came, his year-*timed* mother said,

in her *youth, his ashes* would already be spread.

His *lying* limits pushed, they underestimate,

his nudes accused, a *yellow* pornographic trait.

Ai booked their *ruined* anti-media station

to sing a *choir's* crux of incarceration,

sang Mao's jagged tune, wrung *west* anticipation,

his face lined nude rows, the Red Book's *rest* creation,

Ai reproduced his cell at half the *hanging* scale.

Accused of tax evasion, foreign *glowing* fans

mailed notes to cover the government's *black night* plans.

Cat Mao, chased paper money airplane's *sweet bird* tail,

as Ai threw notes through *boughs*, over patio wall,

the cat would bat, he'd laugh, on film *twilight* they'd fall.

World War III Museum   (128)

When visiting World War II's *living* Museum,

remember *concord* carnage honored, glorified,

quick *nimble* weapons, medals worn for battle's hymn,

with tickets torn for old world's *harvest* rectified.

Brave souls fought battles, *reaped* the war's great prize,

democracies of freedom, *motion* picture gains,

earned monuments like *leaping* beacons to the skies,

all welcomed, terrestrial *gentle* aliens.

The watchers of the skies *bless* how wisdom grows,

observe our kind in *situations* quarantined,

earth's technical childhood *envy* stands, courage throws

new treaties for *blessed* monuments war machined.

An island near Earhart's *bold* landed South Sea rut

holds World War III's museum *stand* in its thatched hut.

Swimming with the Great White Whale   (122-124)

1

It takes a Moby Dick of *memory* to dive,

import the full mathematic fathoms to survive

heart stopped darkness, one's blind spot through *ranked* eyes,

curved by *oblivion's* awed "O" of moon's sunrise.

Corona bent sunset in a *long* deep jump,

unknown if touched down or the whale's *missed* hump?

Ahab stood on his polished whalebone *record* stump,

forgot safe harbors with a whirlwind's *tallied* trump.

To sail the world with *brain* obscured & gory,

collecting sacrifice *scores,* counting scars,

remembering what waves *receive* the story,

he *boldly* struck out for the deep dark's blinding stars,

far shore's bright coast, turned *tables* to reach there,

so far away, until *eternity* from here.

2

The white whale shadows sky's *present* complexion

as clouds of *pyramid* fog rise before the storm,

to witness sailors' sense of *strange* direction,

desires to glisten in glissandos, sea shore foam.

Mannasseh sees Ahab's *continual* stabbing,

luxurious white meat among crisscrossed *old* ropes,

on whale back, wounds roil red with *mighty* jabbing,

dressing his polished whalebone stump to balance hopes

of black & blue *vows* in white water's *scything* slash,

Ahab's *wonder* grins beatifically at last,

a *hasty* guillotine of white whale teeth gnash,

he *boasts*, "The coast can be claimed *new* land this fast!"

He wakes to snarling whales *heard* under the bed,

from coffee cup, mother's *lies*, what the doctor said.

3

His mind swims laps around Starbuck's *state* skull,

adrenalin pools in *time's* dive fathoms deep,

leg tangled harpoon *hate*, rope thrown smash cruel,

awaits the snap *gathered* in the whale's dragged down sleep.

No *fortune's* captive *accident* dream mystery,

enthralled with discontent he swims up the *Thames*

through each thread of liquid *fashioned* tapestry

where what's first *dyed for goodness* next bleaches hymns.

The most incomprehensible *politic* tales

of a universe *unfathered*, Einstein muttered

as *heretic policy* rode atomic whales,

witnessed its wonders comprehensibly *numbered*.

At *Time's* gravity mixer, *hours* stir & shake

pulled bloody spears from the *drowned* heart of Moby Dick.

[Epiphany Crown for Bob Dylan's Noble Prize]

for Martin Jenkins

Big Bang Nutshell Time

1 Stephen Hawking's M-theory of Everything

Unfolding soul shrouds extra dimension access,

awaits our optical solution equations,

set problems calculate artificial success,

held currents move in law compactifications.

Passed depth, height, width, time's six other dimensions stand,

accounts level out the multiverse playing field,

compactified planet staged in a grain of sand

unnoticeable in infinite space-time yield.

Like trachyons appear first as shadow before light,

colliding particles, string theory graviton

moves double gravity while pulsing beyond sight

with particle super-partner symmetry on.

Nutshell Big Bang cellular twist-folds merge as one,

as pairs of eyes do always on some horizon,

2 Redundant Pyramids: Cydonia / Cairo

Crop circles fold tetrahedrons' Merkaba field,

19.5 degrees of latitude displays

Cydonia Martian sphinx face's attitude yield,

designs of extraterrestrial grand arrays.

The pareidolia gaze on Orion's Belt,

exact alignment with Giza pyramid tops,

Cydonia pyramid ruins, Martian melt

of structures conform to Golden Mean space-time spots.

Embedded patterns of Gaia's sacred lights,

"Earth's Grid," Hugh Newman found, 19.5 degrees,

conforms to add hyper dimensional sites,

light's chariot of macro / micro God decrees.

Al–Qahirah, Cairo, "Mars the victorious,"

Egyptians saw Mars as horizon sky's Horus.

3 Galactic Origami Soul

Brain surface grows folds from its core to inner sight

the way tri-horn beetle wings unfold then seek flight.

The Big Bang gravities gather dark matter turns

from micro to macro repeating patterns.

Amino acids, 20, to multitude bones,

attack disease with protein keys, unlock control,

DNA unfolds genetic Rosetta Stones

on cellular levels, origami of soul.

Love's gesture in a nutshell with oyster pearl eye

reflects a blood wolf moon like a scab in the sky

contracts a sign of doom's eclipse emersion,

eclipses double helix entangled vision,

the starlings' murmuration origami cloud

caught up portending a galactic throbbing shroud.

The nut-shelled Big Bang's cellular twist-fold explodes,

a hexagram sequence of souls turns what unfolds.

Lux Volupté's Calm Harbor   (67)

Society plays *living's vein* of *grace*,

lux time notes press, voluptuous space *laced* refrains,

proud lively tunes, a multitude of *lives* in peace...

the lyre *paints nature's infectious* rhythmic *gains*.

One *day* composed from everyday *now* closed,

love's harbor over laid shimmer of *rosiness*,

rewards *she stored* in the rich shiny posed

reflected *blushing* frets, nude sunset bliss.

What she doesn't *steal* from lightning's electric cry,

impiety chimes as the thirteenth of never,

moon's constant *shadowed* face returns the answer why

advantages in each *hue should live* forever.

Her naked *beauty's presence imitates* the *rose*,

bleeds twilight's ultraviolet calm rainbows...

Mother's Spirit (63)

They each took turns & curled *against* her side

as she lay on her last bed's *time* to fly,

her sons & daughters, one by one *fortified*

by her goodness, their goodness to *fortify*

as she lay *vanishing* to take the sky

to welcome *beauty's* liberated spirit,

receive her *travel* well to shrouded cloud's bright eye,

embraced with *age*, her sacred *King* to clear it.

A soul's *sweet* child returned to her children

from end to end, *love's* unending *sight* that bends

back through them over *memory* back again,

as steady, *never cut*, what *love* contends.

You'll want her there in your last *hour's* descent,

to brush the *lines & wrinkles* out, shake up ascent.

for Guy Charleville

Keats Homesick for England (*Endymion, IV*) (129)

Rapt in deep prophetic *spirit* solitude,

loftiest *action* muse! Muse of my native land!

There came an eastern voice of solemn *trusted* mood,

then sang The Nine, Apollo's *extreme* Garland.

Come, sister of the island, the *rude* thing is done

which went undone, these *past* days sooner risen

in barren soul's last flesh *possession* prison.

This I divined with glory, cried *mad* in vain,

adieu dear England's *past* pursuits, her pleasant fields.

Ah, *woeful* me, that I in *bliss* should fondly part,

yet would have her lost *hunted* grapes in sour yields,

my native land's lament, English *world*, foolish heart!

Endymion in *heaven's* dreamed airy dome,

new native air— let me but die from *bloody* Rome!

A Sect of One (*Plus One*) (143)

Lo, hoped for human muse, mentor the *mothered* gun

your life had stood, a harbinger *creature's* touchstone,

a talisman's *reprise*, Jung's *running* "sect of one,"

her words *cried* sermons, transcendental Dickinson.

Inclusion in a double-*catch dispatch* with *you*,

to know *you* in the carriage *pursuit* next *to me*,

two couplets *hold your neglected* garden in view,

the horse heads neigh *bent* to *face* the oak & posy.

The circled coming *stay*, forever *busy* full,

entirely for Shakespeare, *crying* in constraints,

where revelations *chase*, ours *fly* the *back turned* tool,

behold *me*, next to *you*, *kiss me*, one of *your* saints.

To stanza-land we hurry, *pray* for *Walt's* same *care*,

your bearings *catch* us up the breathless *turn*, Will's share.

This antique book *returns* to great psalm's grace

when *bent* to each one, ambient to each ones place

as written in the quick of a *catching* heart,

not far *behind* words *prayed* to *quicken* future art.

The *child-like* hand that curved a holy specter's mind,

two points' perspective into the future shined.

Whether troubadour's *loud* warble or David's tale

unbound to *chase* the secret in the thunder's bell,

until the shepherd's flock through new madrigals *fly*,

embrace her *housewife cares*, *kind face* with *kindest* eye.

Haunted Generation 2

1 Quantum Entanglement

If *seeing* it changes it, when is it real

or *broken* in a throw of quantum dice?

Two people separate, distance identical,

one particle influences the other, *twice*...

same *constancy* travels faster than light,

unlimited *blindness,* then to reappear,

the same equation's *enlightenment* right,

a quantum point *bearing* access right here...

We *vowed* in the same world's symmetrical bell

that rang through Germany's *foresworn* classroom door,

till I arrived *unknown* at her White Sands neighbor

years later...again, Susan's *truth* wed me to tell...

a Tao of parallels in the physics of *things,*

remotely *sworn* for future, quantum's system clings...

Truth reaffirms change, psyche's regeneration,

unmasked *faith-torn* trial's haunted generation.

2 Heavenly Dream World: First Level

Susan's *faith* rewound, resurrection Sabbath morn

after three days, *honest* dream, Guy's visitation,

her busy *bearing*, our *new* house separation,

had to ask how she liked it, to check scorn once *sworn*.

Among her beautiful *loved things* not to forget,

Guy's *truth* smiled from his resurrected body

& *loved* us with a baby elephant pet,

artful on the sofa so we'd rub its belly.

Then Guy & I walked on paths by fields *vowing* wheat,

to steep high footbridge, a *deep* stream under our feet

led to schoolyard cheer, *enlightened* students to greet,

new classroom windows large streamed wisdom's *kind* retreat.

Truth reaffirmed change, psyche's regeneration,

unmasked *faith-torn* trial's haunted generation.

3 Her Next Life Visitation

Framed dreams lined up like *vowed* series of thoughts

bearing layers, departing, *new* destinations,

degrees of parted *loved* ones, couldn't & could knots,

in *honest* labyrinths, sequenced tabulations.

Deep oath as married, once divorced, in after death

unaltered *love* light's constant justification,

before death's *act* sorts truer kinds of breath,

black void *breached* to *new* visionary union.

The angels *know* we'll peer through dark, search light's region,

enlightened work on the fielded dream's completion;

beside the counter, tall bookshelves, *kind* perfect wife,

stands unconditional *love's* resurrected life!

Truth reaffirms change, psyche's regeneration,

unmasked *faith-torn* trial's haunted generation.

for Guy & Susan

Yeats' Last Paradigm Vision

They lay in love, that first day of new sun,

had seen each other once in one day's dawn,

her face, something of sun, held everyone

enthralled to poetry, no need be drawn

for image making, so-and-so would come

to populate with ease of garden birth,

where all but one fruit's never cumbersome,

ecstatic copulations, steady mirth!

No shriven courtesy, love's holograph,

no need to read, quote/unquote learned books,

as nothing idle, all shines free enough.

Colloquial stars, invitation looks

contained raptures, diametrical tunes,

each celebrated phases of new moons.

Her Unburdened Prescience   (65)

Her spirit writes the better part of her *power*

consuming light, her words long *mortal* composure,

the other side of sleep, *beauty* waking over

dreams flowing shades deep, double *wracked* exposure.

The dual *day*, word-winded *restful* prescient breath,

like smoke rises, a *honey* consciousness incense.

Her words refuse *impregnable* ravages, death,

with montage eye, rye rabbi, suspense *black ink* sense.

Her poems, a mother's well prepared *jeweled* nest,

for milking kindness nurtured *time-chest* waterlines.

Her eyes shined *meditation's* philosopher test,

wisdom's gemstones of eternal *miracle* signs.

Unburdened by death, lines dig, *decay*, exhume,

replant the love of her words, *shine bright* to full bloom.

for Maxine Cassin

Lin Emery Circle's Cursive Flight   (108)

Flight's orbital edge wings its *figured* lives,

rotating sky fins like wielding *spirit* knives,

a shrine's *divine* suspense for palm, lily pad pond,

carves dragonfly mist, turns banana's *hallowed* frond.

The arch in the oak limb curves to *count* a star,

presages lunar half-*days* from where we are.

Flight's *prayer* to magnolia bloom, lotus blossom,

to balance eagle wing, *antiquity* contained,

flies future's *wrinkle* through fluid aluminum,

the *character* of wind's eclipse attained.

The wingtip dips invisible *ink* to eye,

imaginary flight in *place* to augur sky

where birds can not fly & *dust* gather inside,

the nest of intuitive landing *weighs* to glide,

a *page's* span, word, phrase, sentence, mission,

expressive action symbol, way of word fission.

Hunched over Notre Dame

The hand made nun's wax spills as covered with his blood,

don't get too close to her gold sling-shot crucifix,

no match lit in the candle shop fire flood,

live wire sparks behind her wall that starts to hiss.

The steeple in a cloud stood upright stout,

above cathedral billows, altar, turned, fell down...

did Jesus framed in rafters just then shout,

grime faced in cubist vestments, neck bent to look out?

No need for crown of thorns, roof nails impaled the same,

a sudden moment shaken down from Notre Dame

held madness, French ladies could not avert their gaze,

turn iPhones from their sad cathedral wrapped in flames.

Good Friday's silenced bell can't rescue what it lacks,

the rafters must be climbed pressed against their hunched backs.

Firefighters stand the blaze crack rumbled thunder,

as thousands of bees still buzz the rooftop beehive,

& billionaires speed to rebuild wages, wonder

how Yellow Jackets on Champs-Élysée survive.

Celestial Accounting with Cubits (148)

Arch pointed, vaulted ceiling, *fault's* flying buttress,

counts faith that built the *fled world's* gothic cathedral.

From sacred numbers God *denotes* the multiverse

& building heaven's *corresponding* vehicle.

The cubit, from elbow to *judgment's* finger tip,

wide 50 cubits, Noah's *cunning* rainbow arc,

then 30, 60, Solomon's *eyed* temple strip,

oraculorum's *censure* cubit measured mark.

What need have we to measure the city *falsely*,

top 144 cubit *watching* walls,

without the wrestled angel ladder's *viewed* pity,

to paradise through doors down *true sight's* halls,

to *marvel* galaxies like Meadowlark Lemon,

till heaven's dome *clears* steps ahead as counted down?

First Man on the Moon   (113)

The man like the moon he walked on, *mind* mystified

of baby Buddha, dust danced, flag *governed* turf,

sequestered, part blind *function*, blast off dignified,

his *vision's* inner swim, salmon's upstream surf.

In early days from mid-west *birds, flowers,* cornfields,

he'd smile beside an X-15's *latch* flight photos.

From sea to shining *mountains,* Gemini hurled yields,

Armstrong, Aldrin and Collins, *left* the protos.

Though Neil's mythology *holds* nothing like Ovid's,

it launched for timely writers the *catch*-words divined,

the Eagle's *heart* landed for Janet and the kids,

one *gentle* step for man's giant leapt mankind.

In ship *shaped* space throwing Einstein's diced up stars,

moon *minds* form payloads, Curiosity for Mars.

Delicate Thunder Embraced Awareness

Delicate thunder softly overwhelmed my ear's

torment, as recollection's amen-corner of

my meditation alignment with what it hears,

distilled scenes, punctuated revelation love.

The next world she'll live better lived in beyond

among attending spirits of the thunder dome

who weigh belled better judgments, little prayers fond,

resounding to hearts deceitful, crooked, rung home.

What justice prevails when her friend's blithe Iago

works rendered Othello's last pillow ordered thrown,

as if the two bad daughters of Lear's overthrow

capitulated clutched kingdom theft's last agon?

The spirits hear me contemplate the action's ends,

with thunder emphasize my phrased accounts of friends.

Apocalyptic Cycle

Thank you for keeping all my truths bound up to wrap,

it caused the questioning of everything till tapped,

how feet move freely without fear of bones that snap

against a floor of concrete sealed deceits entrapped.

The visionary dreams unchosen by reason,

truth's due given extremes to measured remedy,

time's weathered personal wear, shared each ones season,

divined to match in other books what's meant to be.

As rituals search out a rightful proving ground,

the reborn visit's glory appeared fully formed

of unconditional love, perfect, no one scorned,

did not view every rite, in fullness stood reformed

with special care for each one's undistracted scope,

contrived dreams carry now more varied doors of hope

to destinations hurried, the same dual goal,

where laid up treasure expounds on homes of renewed soul.

Guy's Revivified Mind

With Guy there was never an unresolved conflict,

his lead example cushioned falling hard knocks,

passed on his nature's open space to connect

with those at odds, how some recalcitrant child talks.

My spots of time with Guy return to every plight

of lifted edges he saw through under each rock

that troubled other teachers' less budging insight.

Guy gave to hapless violent souls kindness to shock

complacency from change if slammed against a wall.

The smiling hands-on approach Guy shares with his wife,

stayed passed on to a friend & kindly led the call,

all hiking to the mountains, renews the good life.

I look toward tough times when thoughts on Guy so kind

with Janice, Vivian, revivify my mind.

Credit where Credit's Due

Discovering faced books online a bit late,

you've heard it, better late than disavowed fate,

better turns to your hegemonic state,

hedged up so fast it doesn't need a past due date

when your future's all thumbs up right here & now,

a great hitch-hiker riding a cosmic tail-gate,

all thumbs one day, then declensions the great debate,

your word *abomination* ..sums up the planned how

deep you strive for presence, to be on the right side,

cast horse-race bet ramifications, do or try,

until they catch up with you, find how to decide

what stretches reason's stance, you teach how to cry.

Your cause as big as Ben Bernanke's saves the world,

at last credit counseling put out fires hurled.

Angel Trumpets

1 All for your Everything (85)

Will you have my all for your *tongue-tied* everything,

convince your skeptic turn *compiled* to ride me out

where nature churns the *reserved* stomach's muscling

in on receiving *precious* signals from the gut?

We were acquainted first through the same *muse's* friends,

returned to *hymns* a *lettered* intimate season.

Determined break from *clerks* on which my *pen* depends,

caused *polished* choice to reconsider chosen.

Few carry me away *hearing* the way you do,

the hunting in your eye still *praises* my twilight,

astonished cares prepared to know this *love for you*,

your *hindsight's* dangerous dark rooms at midnight.

Break through tomorrow's Roman holiday *respects*,

high mission morning's impossible way *effects*.

2 Time Heals, Wounds to Heal (86)

Time takes the distillation of its *proud* effects

to new *bound* depths poured through a precious past,

night's undertow that falls with *rehearsed* affects,

shrunk present moving upstream, *verse entombed* at last.

Time's not Love's fool, hands cannot clutch *spirit* seconds

then envy loss, her captive *mortal* numbered face.

Tell love a thing or two of *night's* demanding ends

beyond the watchman's *lines* calling out dawn's burnt pace,

bound up clocks speared by shaken *ghostly* times,

each day's half-cut worn *nightly* weathered blue surprise.

The hungered *victor's* beaten counts of hollow crimes,

rewound spring *fears*, self-wounds *sickness* personifies.

The clock-face world *filled*, every *lifeline* unwound

as hours pass, unwinds what *matters*, heals the wound.

3 Spirit Guide   (87)

Consuming life's last quadrant, *farewell's* last wound,

to Simon's Rome, *charter* Dr. Bloom as Virgil,

set up discovery *bonds*, pass exiled contents bound.

Feed deep on *granted* forces waiting in the Grail,

mine caves for *riches*, noble canon fodder,

explode *sleep* darkness with *determining* art,

aligned to *swerve* Galileo's alma mater,

illuminating navigation's *knowing* chart.

Perceived at times more clearly *given* bright in *dreams*,

imagination *misprision* fired, heaven slakes,

quenched where extended *better judgment* teems.

With shadowed faces, *estimate* their marks...

when hewing mind's eye, *knowing's* canonical

possessing heresy's *waking* gnostic temple.

4 Incarnadine Mind   (88)

Time's sprung, *disposed* in a blossomed rose-wound temple,

encrypted springs to *merit* first selected leads,

their diagram, DNA's *vantage* point *double*,

proves *bending* moon's eclipse corona bleeds

out curving edges, *set* rose-gold, haloes circle,

dual wheels inner *gain* for second crown's sharper thorns,

twined *virtuous* vined helix, geared cyclical

to *injured* going of a Fisher King's returns.

A Passover sunset's *scornful* golden aspect,

incarnadine pearl mother's *love-light* horizon

on *tainted* moon's first shell, pink pearl cloud duet,

low galleon cloud leans, *concealed* tether to sun.

The lake soon *parts* a *losing* skyline blotted dark,

the *eye of storm*, moon as earth's *forsworn* ark.

5 Divined Family   (89)

Where Dante's exile *forsakes* Beatrice' arc,

hears Solomon's song *defend* newer testament,

his *tongue* no longer *reasoned* artifice as dark,

new wine's *acquaintance* flask, old skin shed sacrament.

She *loves* the *will* of messianic vision,

rose blossomed mindful mother's *beloved* peace

from ages *old* where middle age looks on

as *loved ones dwell* where futures *will* not cease.

When entering tomorrow's *desired* rest

between the covering wings to *tell* ark angels,

her *name* beatified curves out his *form* the best,

resets the bonds sustaining *debated* angles.

Was better he'd been born *vowed* to be exiled,

than ever see her *hating* her imperfect child.

/

41

6 Great Catch (90)

His loaves served the *windswept world's* wayward child,

rain stopper, lake walker, bread basket diplomat,

across set tables *woeful* enemies schemed wild,

he fished for fishers, future *fortune's* habitat.

Three days of anguish swallowed *loss* like Jonah's shock,

escaped to beach with friends & feast on *fortune's* fish,

spared *grief's spite*, *left* with interstellar Enoch,

to build their parallel mansions, *strain* planned anguish.

When whale oil *last* stretched *nights* in the temple lamp,

the *worst* of light was veiled, *lingered* for the Romans

whose siege below *conquered* walls would not break camp

until cursed stones *came down* to fill omens.

The woman at his *deeds* last supper broke bread,

compared first counted loaves & fish debris point spread.

7 Body's Heir   (91)

Some glory in manifesting destiny's spread,

poetic long *skills*, primed subversive ends,

when heard what curse to move his bone's *rest* would be said,

the broken stones fit back where *adjunct* work contends.

Control the stomach to *garment* the soul

like Parsifal's quest fielding new green *richer* corn,

the *body*, spirit, mind, *alone*, *wealth* of the whole,

to be as *measured*, born for *body's force* reborn.

Attentive rings rhymed of a *general* sonneteer,

yields *humor's* echo, *proud love's* thorough *bettered* year,

finds life's short lease fitted for *higher* views,

returns remembrance of cost, *pleasured* dues.

Well tempered with *new-fangled ill's* glad sorrowing,

will you have my *all* for your tongue-tied everything?

Ancestral Aliens (153)

They know my little faith accounts for *kindling* time,

to be there while I'm *fired* up *quickly* in here

anticipating an exo-*love* requiem

in momentary depths to peer *love's holy fire*.

Distempered malady no longer fears *sovereigns*,

their hard drives *seething* with what I dream about,

no overbearing conjured *desire* persuasions,

a few bad movies geared their science *trial* rout.

Mapped out proceeds divined a *sickness* circuitry,

they know my knowing's versed to *cure* for business sake.

Convivial ones *brand sleep*, carry me away,

a chance to turn to *fountains* of Melchizedek.

Without their harbinger *valley's* destiny,

till fully theirs, my *strange* paradox *proves* lonely.

If memory's *bath* can *endure* the *dateless* pale,

new fire will soon part Vivian's heavenly veil.

ASAP: Age of Second Adam's Paradigm

The wings of birds in flight, the ideal smile
of Leonardo's resurrected pointing John,
the finger painted Mona's, never out of style,
reveals self-knowledge, deflects ones prison archon.
Preparing for the final conflict's cosmic seam,
Blue Turbaned Prince, Persian devouring Beast,
twilight adjacent time, twixt waking thought & dream,
angelic blessing for the coming written feast...
A six-string medley of three songs cascade,
to tall oaks as their inner flight rose in song,
a choir of birds chime flourishes to chiming played,
a sect of one's oracle lifts the song along.
Passed winged words parting on a razor's edge
while contemplating angels from a mountain ledge
who travel deep in valleys for a second look
between the pages fading of a mission book,
the end returns Pleroma's unfallen fullness,
to find us resting there in perpetual bliss.

Under the Orbital Lilac Tree

Between the lines' material, chasing the moon

his Kosmos calls from an orbital lilac tree,

its taproot tallying the orbs of destiny

as I lie in glowing fields, dream up his night's tune.

To watch him gaze at stars, the same wrapt everything,

no old man here from timeless aspirations fled,

his daylight transcendental smile, Kosmic thinking

eclipses earth with other moons where death has sped

like night-birds to her virtue's inward sunshine eye,

content perfection's inherited grace

as sudden ease of focus pulls love in to fly

desire's sweetest lines, drawn to her sovereign face.

Why would love happen not at death's call of beauty?

There'll be no "no's" for you not to know no pity.

A Unified Field Ballad

To touch fingers of nature's hidden hand

spells out in numerological laws,

the warp & weft of sky relative to land

& how ground gravitates in space-time's clause.

Why does the hydrogen atom not radiate

like Mercury spinning around the sun,

as geometry's warps & curves calculate

the ever accelerating creation?

The black hole error turned against curvature

within blackout moonstone's sarcophagus roll,

stone tossed ripple's mathematical architecture

shows up lastly where time elapsed, to slower soul,

the great equation of unification,

eternity's passed future enumeration...

Appendix 1

Fields of Dreams: Symbols of Consciousness

As "Leaves of Grass," Walt Whitman named his expanding book with a metaphorical and allusive title. "Leaves," pages of his poems, stretches from noun to verb for how grass grows and withers in a cycle of nature, appearing then leaving, then reappearing, etc. The noun-verb alludes to four Psalms (37:2, 90:5-6, 103:15, 102:4) and several New Testament passages with the grass metaphor on the nature of human life. One may Google for proof of his title's transcendental aspect. Although more thorough at times than the mind, there is no artificial consciousness in Google.

Dr. Harold Bloom in the *Leaves of Grass,* 150th anniversary 1[st ed.] reprint intro, refers to the "Whitman sublime" being unsurpassed among modern English language poets with only Emily Dickinson coming close (p. xvi). Dr. Bloom identifies the "paradigm" of Whitman's sublime as the *King James Bible* with Walt's essential poetics marked by the translations of William Tyndale and Miles Coverdale (p. xxii). He goes on to examine where Walt's American sensibilities were filtered through the transcendental lens of Ralph W. Emerson's essays such as: *The Over-Soul; Spiritual Laws* and *The Poet,* as if Whitman reflected Emerson's major ideas that ignited imagination. If Walt's sublime as individual prophet of a new American love religion issued from Emerson's harbinger prose, Dr. Bloom finds it in the essays where Emerson calls on the "method-men" as "symbols of consciousness" (p. xxiii). This is what resonates with Whitman to fill the "poet-void" Emerson describes in *The Poet.*

Google's artificial intelligence, not consciousness, searches unlike autonomous self-driving cars, as that skillset's current jargon uses a new word, "roadmanship," based on driver road safety measures, according to *Wired* magazine (3/2019 p. 19). The same *Wired* issue, the essay, *Alexa, I want Answers,* by James Vlahos (p. 59) on "voice computing," shares challenges seeking "the one perfect response to any question" from how answers may rank upwardly on the knowledge response chain. This leads to imagine new word creations like "truthmanship," "questmanship," etc. A closer step toward Star Trek suggests "Scotty, beam me the answer."

The voice-computing article opens and closes with thoughts on the work of William Tunstall-Pedoe, who created what led to the Echo & "Alexa" and how after leaving Amazon in 2016, he "acknowledges that voice oracles introduce new risks, or at least worsen existing ones" ...these problems can be solved by "better technology... AIs that learn to suppress factually incorrect info" (p. 67) ...perhaps in a way that his software, Anagram Genius, helped Dan Brown " generate "plot-critical puzzles" in *The Da Vinci Code* (p. 61).

A correctness measure may one day be called "truthmanship" in bearing artificially intelligent research across media applications. The word could apply to human thought processes and the outcome of reasoning in how Vlahos (p. 61) says "Search engines as helpful librarians... must eventually yield to AIs as omniscient oracles." As verification measures are applied to truth in various digital media accounts, a current contention, to near paranoia, is suggested by Zeynep Tufekci in the *Wired* issue (p. 19): "Every verification method carries the threat of surveillance."

When self-directed surveillance involves a transcendentalist poet like Whitman, engaged in his era's journalism for several years, as a reader of the classics and serious contemporaries such as Emerson, the efforts resulted in poems like "Song of Myself" and the entire scope of *Leaves of Grass*. Ezra Pound surveyed it as having "one sap and one root" with him, though it was Walt who, he wrote, had "broke the new wood" of which Pound wanted "carving" and shared "commerce."

Would it seem odd to Professor Bloom who deemed Emerson "our John the Baptist" with Walt "certainly the American literary Christ" (L/G intro p. xxxiii) to find me considering Walt's Psalm allusions in what may be one of the most non-paranoid grand poetics ever written in English?

The self-surveillance in *Leaves of Grass* may also remind one of a New Testament story (John 1: 45-49) (not to take considerations away from the Gnostic *Gospel of Thomas*.) When Philip told Nathanael who had not yet met Jesus that here was the one the old prophets wrote of, Nathanael asked if anything good could come out of Nazareth. Upon meeting, Jesus declared him a true Israelite in whom there is no guile, to which Nathanael asked how did he know him. Jesus related that he observed Nathanael under a fig tree before Philip found him, apparently without the knowledge of those there, to which Nathanael exclaimed verification of Jesus as King of Israel and his Lord. The observation amounts to surveillance Nathanael sees as non-threatening or could it be good-threatening? Jesus then tells Nathanael he shall see greater things such as heaven open and angels ascending and descending. Could what happened under the fig tree have something to do with an angel? It does not say, but sensibilities are heightened due to compact details engaged in "truthmanship" that sets up faith in what is not yet seen based on former surveillance.

There is little doubt that Walt Whitman understood deep useful intelligence was rooted in an attitude of faith and earned through experience. The appearance of idleness and glorious hard physical work, this dual attitude, is presented as the front print in *Leaves of Grass* by Whitman's stance, right fist on hip tilt, left hand in pants pocket, head tilt, hat cocked to the side, relaxed man of action, seriously gazing at the viewer to come to grips with truth.

The trilogy, *Shakespeare AI*, took shape from sonnet forms with rules of content and container to become a vehicle for expressions of life mysteries. A writer friend challenged me to write sonnets and others encouraged continuing them. There have been writer friends who belittled the idea at best and even mocked or ridiculed the notion, implying that while perhaps conversing with Shakespeare, it had no relevance to them or current serious writing in our time, being as obsolete as a useless antique. Nevertheless, I built a book of sonnets allowed to multiply, divide and change over 15 years that involved essay and letter writing before coming to its own completion.. not knowing this last expanse of writing would involve the shocking deaths of Guy Charleville, a dearest teacher co-worker friend and my beloved Susan, librarian ex-wife. I had hoped the book would somehow help absolve me in her eyes.

As expected, after their deaths in less than a month, Dec. 21, 2018 his, and hers, Jan. 12, 2019, a series of dreams came, followed by poems and the realization that the reactions to these poems and dreams through an exchange of letters with my theatrical singer friend, Diana, who two years prior had lost her husband, Wesley, spurred the need to write. The new poems give the book a more profound completion in a planned 4th volume, *Radio Waves for the Blind*. YouTube video interviews on life after death with hypnotherapist Dolores Cannon, shared comparable dream events in line with some experiences in the trilogy. There remain things she accepted in her broad range of "truthmanship" after working for 40 years regressing clients through passed lives as subconscious conduits to spirit realm personalities working out karma issues, I clearly can not yet abide with due to atonement & forgiveness.

Volume 1, *Shakespeare's Wake*, began and resolved with dreams; 1st: a night's angelic visitation, while in bed seeming to be dreamily awake, aware of the room and lying there, feet toward the window, she end's up placing my resting left hand on my heart as if to quickly consecrate a writer; 2: In an epilogue poem, my adopting army dad appeared wonderfully in another most lucid realistic dream. The poem *Resurrection Visitation* expands on it with Shakespeare sonnet (151) allusions:

> "*Content* internal radiance like fire baptized,
> he left *me* waking to *his* death defect as *prized*."

An awesome blessing, its joyous seriousness spread curious delight, calm in afterlife observations among diverse people in a new/old city. The reunion, visited by Dad as my guide from an army clapboard clinic door, on a ramp to a huge grand old brownstone busy church-like porch. He stepped down smiling to greet my awe and show me among fine youthful men and women, another similar brownstone, letting me enter, look around see its surface renovation work in the entry room, kind men working calmly, then in an empty fine hall leading to rooms where I alone, not yet prepared to go, chose to return to him on the sidewalk. He left, no look back, bounded up the stairs in his perfect green fatigues and boots, to a new porch and gently slipped through the partially opened door, ending the dream.

Volume two, *Recycling the Circle*, deals with social, political, cultural, psychological, scientific and philosophical modern issues and contains as many prints as poems. While structuring and formatting material the death of Stephen Hawking happened from which an extended sonnet came. This gave the book an ending relative to some advanced scientific thought and physics jargon of the day.

It opens with a sonnet on the idea of Dr. Martin Luther King Jr. and Abraham Lincoln sharing a double memorial. A sonnet competing with a monument was proposed by Shakespeare in his Sonnet 55. Two sonnets and more later enlarged the series for a chapbook. In one sonnet sequence, *Redundant Pyramids*, pertains to Martian forms aligned in relation to pyramids of Giza and Orion star groupings. The third sonnet of this "epiphany crown," *Galactic Origami Soul*, blends modern science with organically mystical nature myths of the soul. The volume 2 cover has Lin Emery's *Flight* sculpture replacing Lee on the monument as in a dream in 2000 and remembered when arriving at Lee Circle that morning while driving Susan to work at the main library. I returned to take photos and plan double exposures to explore the dream at length, over several months, many rolls of film and lots of sketches. Gradually a series of prints added to the B&W volume 2 and became a plan for a large format color edition.

Volume three, *Romance Languages*, started as a comedic parody on the muses Shakespeare frequently engaged with in his sonnets. It has a composite picture of Susan from behind at a Mardi Gras float raising her hands to catch a Rex throw on Canal Street in the late 90's. The cover collage title is *Grasping the Unattainable*. Most of the illustrations in the current set up are elegant parodies of Leonardo da Vinci's main depicted ladies in drawings and paintings, all with wine glasses, at Stonehenge for the "First Picnic" which is also intended as a satire of Dan Brown's book, *The Da Vinci Code*. Monty Python's Terry Gilliam was also a bit influential.

On her condo couch, I showed Susan different versions of the volumes with illustrations. It was her first evening out of the hospital after chemo and radiation therapy was completed and the same day, but we did not know then, that Guy was killed in a car wreck as a passenger in his own Honda Civic, the same death trap car, as I've heard it called, that was owned by Susan.

Susan's condition deteriorated in the next few days with low blood pressure and dehydration to the point where the doctor ordered her return. Her friend Tony called on the morning of Jan. 12 and said Susan was rushed from a nursing home recovery to the emergency room with chest pains where she was pronounced dead. On Jan. 14th I received a card from Janice, Guy's wife, thanking me for the trilogy where she found the poem written for Guy on the death of his mother, she wrote she would keep it and me close to her heart.

Two nights before Susan died, *Einstein's Quantum Riddle* was shown on PBS, a vivid dream followed with Susan and Guy that helped stop my bedtime weeping for a while. More expected dreams came that were noted while researching several books, the internet, YouTube videos and while writing two "epiphany crowns." *Haunted Generation 2*, fit the trilogy's expanded ending as *Big Bang Nutshell Time* fleshed out volume two's ending. Altogether the series held plans for a chapbook sequence.

Guy and Susan looked their best in the dreams ..no words recalled, they seemed delighted being there. Susan in her pre-death dream looked superb in casual elegant light pastel pants and long sleeved top in our stately white two story New Orleans manor with shiny cherry-rosewood floors, cream walls, with soft accented shadows in corners. Clear amber tinged light streamed through an open window's white sheer breezy curtains at the far side of the spacious living room, while bright outside from other angles. Verbally subdued, busy with beautiful household objects and modern furniture, moving from the kitchen, as a cat wandered by to other rooms, Susan didn't pay much attention to me. I had to ask how she liked this place, implied as compared to the previous places we lived in that she didn't care much for. She showed her interest as if it were a rhetorical question, obvious to see, while she kept busy turned to fine new things with no conversation.

Guy rounded the driveway by a tall hedge and nicely edged grassy front yard, dressed in a dapper deep olive/green hiking outfit. I met him dressed as usual, neat Ralph Lauren Polo double pocket dark shirt and tan chinos as on beautiful days when we taught middle school Special Ed. boys and girls at Eisenhower Elementary. He was happy to greet me, as if after a long journey, returned from a great distance. Going inside to see Susan and the house, we checked out three sweet cats, then Guy suddenly surprised us in the living room from a hallway with a baby pet elephant that acted like a big puppy climbing on a chair then rolled around next on the sofa for a belly rub. This playful greeting was a lot of fun for all of us. After that Guy and I went out a side patio door to a grassy yard walkway to a lane by rows of fine two story houses, then a field by a stream with a high footbridge, down to houses before a newly renovated high tech industrial building for a school on the neighborhood outskirts by fields.

Arriving at the site we met a group of delightfully eager middle school students in the yard. Girls & boys lined up casually, chatting while waiting to enter the building. Guy and I entered a side door on a wide hall that led to our new large well-appointed classroom with tables, computers and film screen. Huge windows let enough light in to make the open space look luminous and transparent throughout. A small group of girls and boys sat at a side table as Guy began casually discussing the day's nature/space science study. I planned visual media and art supplies for the subject while observing them. All were delighted to be there for this learning reunion as if every day from then on would be "Happy Earthday" in and beyond school.

After waking from the dream there came a sense of relief about Guy, just as when dad appeared in the dream revealing his revitalized new life after death as we know it, to graciously share a welcoming glimpse of this glorious new state. Dad and Guy both appeared in their job context from life.

My long time actor, filmmaker, singer, talent-teacher friend Diana, had commented on the first improved version of the book I gifted her. She found large parts of it difficult to comprehend and realized its tedious task to complete. She wanted to help with the book by generously offering to pass it on to her editor uncle. It needed work on continued updates and improvements before someone tried to wrap a mind around it.

While musing on the similarities and contrasts of poems with documentary films, my friend Paulette sent a link to the critic Roger Ebert's essay on Werner Herzog films that linked to an interview with Herzog. Roger said, "He is willing to push beyond documentary fact... in his quest for underlying truth... Herzog moves freely through spheres of fact, fiction, legend, myth and invention." At the Telluride interview with Roger on Sept. 29, 1998, Werner said, "The weakness of cinema verite' documentaries is that they can not go any deeper. They can only reach the surface of what constitutes truth in cinema. Deeper truth can only be found in poetry, because then you start to fabricate. The world is simply there. It is what men find in it and bring to it that is truth. I am in search of the fathomless." Roger wrapped it up with, "It takes art, the arranging and adjusting, to fashion someone else's experience into our own."

I thought of Diana's quest to complete her documentary after Wesley's death two years earlier and wondered how much these ideas figured into her efforts. She read my new poems that came as I began to process the deaths of Guy and Susan. It was touching and illuminating to get her feedback. She intuitively wanted to clarify my efforts and help by considering the epiphany crown's first of three sonnets word for word and line by line.

The time-saddled methods of the process, allowing the poem, and book, to show how to proceed over time required subconscious and conscious links to visualize what leads to completion. Links, like allusions, a conduit for imagination, play a crucial role in the work's development. Language use was for an enrichment of imaginative experience in trusting the higher reaches of subconscious mind while at times recognizing when dipping into the pool of universal unconscious mind. The mind should be allowed to wander, even fail as Jeff Bezos, among others, has said in group motivational meetings.

 After awhile Diana responded with a detailed account of parsing the first poem for meaning and asked for clarifications in the following relaxed, non-critical, complementary way.. here is the poem revised a bit first:

Haunted Generation 2 (Shakespeare Sonnet 152 allusions in italics)

1 Quantum Entanglement

If *seeing* it changes it, when is it real

or *broken* in a throw of quantum dice?

Two people separate, distance identical,

one particle influences the other, *twice*…

same *constancy* travels faster than light,

unlimited *blindness,* then to reappear,

the same equation's *enlightenment* right,

a quantum point *bearing* access right here…

We *vowed* in the same world's symmetrical bell

that rang through Germany's *foresworn* classroom door,

till I arrived *unknown* at her White Sands neighbor

years later… again, Susan's *truth* wed me to tell…

55

a Tao of parallels in the physics of *things*,

remotely *sworn* for future, quantum's system clings…

Truth reaffirms change, psyche's regeneration,

unmasked *faith-torn* trial's haunted generation.

In reading this Haunted Generation 2 - I really liked it.

As I don't know what everything means, I wrote down what I believe

you mean and ask for clarification. Thanks.

So for fun and as a challenge to me, tell me how close am I

to understanding. Haunted Generation: (Sins of our families, fathers,

that carry down from generation to generation)

If seeing it changes it, when is it real - I Love this!

Dictionary defines Quantum as any of the very small increments or

parcels into which many forms of energy are subdivided" and dice as:

a gambling game played. Can you - for clarification please, tell me

what you mean by "broken in a throw of quantum dice

Two people separate, distance identical - (I love this!)

unlimited blindness then to reappear, (This means both parties continue

to not "see" –each other, or their relationship, the others' needs, etc

One particle influences the other, (love this) twice

Same constancy travels faster than light, (The constancy of what?)

"Unlimited blindness then to reappear, (love this)

the same equation's enlightenment right, " (What does this mean to you,

please?" a quantum bearing accessed as right here... (an increment

providing an opening?) She and I vowed in the symmetrical bell ringing

in Germany's foresworn classroom. (You met in Germany, at school,

and married to the ringing of wedding bells)

arriving at her White Sands unknown neighbor's home (White Sands, a

town, and "unknown neighbor's home," someone who lived near by and

she didn't know them years later, late again, Susan's truth out to tell...

a Tao of parallels in universal things. (timing was off, yet Susan speaks

her truth and opinions of general life matters.) remotely sworn for future

(Things she vowed to continue to share years

earlier) quantum's system cling's (?) Truth reaffirms change,

psyche's regeneration, (thus, the "Entanglement")

unmasked fear- (love this) torn trial's haunted generation. (the haunted

legacy left after life's trials torn by courage to face and show one's fear.

The poet John Keats came to a concept like an attitude he named as "Negative Capability" that could stimulate expansion of consciousness for the imagination considering poetic constructs. In a letter to a friend he said the idea worked as a literary ingredient, an attitude of acceptability to "be in doubts and ambiguities" for a deeper imaginative experience of poetry than just the surface intentions of literal meaning. Keats mentioned Shakespeare possessed large quantities of Negative Capability throughout the plays, including the sonnets, which reveals and needs a reader's "tour de force" of Negative Capability to fully engage the imagination.

Here begins the parsing of Diana's parsing: her last statement resonates the most imaginative experience, "life's trials torn by courage" where she tries to parse the title "Haunted Generation," while not "seeing" psychological layers of experience reflected by "2." A "haunting" can be involuntary returns, something generated" as a caused experience and can be cyclical in a "generational" aspect.

Part 1, *Quantum Entanglement*, is a physics concept unseen to the naked-eye based on scientific equations, post-event observation or conjectured activity with a theory of quantum particles, so small the thing is "there but not there" to perception where the observation itself effects it. This mysterious event, like briefly glimpsed symbols moving in a minute (yet vast) scaled atomic universe, another symmetrical aspect of reality, combined with the outer or larger universe, is what Einstein might refer to as "General Relative Infinity."

Hauntings and generations belong to the human experience in how human entanglements manifest. One may Google the overlapping connection of quantum physics studies with paranormal psychic experiments to get a sense of the possibilities in esoteric physics phenomena.

The PBS network's 1-9-19, Nova documentary, *Einstein's Quantum Riddle*, also seemed to haunt me. That night I dreamed of Guy's visit to Susan and I in a beautiful house before she died on Saturday morning, Jan. 12th. I watched the film, noted some ideas and alluded to them in *Haunted Generation*, line 1: "If seeing it changes it, when is it real?" The rhetorical question answers itself: at each moving change or level "it" is real. The origin of my experience with Susan developed in tangents only to return to the mysterious relationship.

The difference in reading poems verses essays is how poetics assist in creative imagination's more diverse experience. Poems may require several readings to develop deeper imaginative elements with aspects that differ from essays, thus we have "poetic license." Though poems may trigger emotion, it may sound like flattery to express love or like for this or that.

Reading with anxiety acceptance can achieve rich diverse imaginative poetic experience. Anxiety of influence, Dr. Harold Bloom's "diagnosis" in his book of that name, relates to a struggle in a poet's work with a previous poet's work influencing the current poet, as in arrangements of words, what was created by the other, in a way that is contended with, compared to, or composed achieving measures of misreading and internal conflict.

One's Negative Capability may start with ambivalence to nailing down assumptions of what a thing is. One may feel imagination grow in time, get to know it as "it" gets to know oneself (in a form of "entanglement"). This is revealed in dramatic monologues and soliloquies of Shakespeare, Hamlet's conflicted "self-inquiries" or Robert Browning's *My Last Duchess*.

Begin reading with ambivalence to ambiguity. With generous spirit "it" prompts open mindedness to creative thinking, which seems to give "powers that be" trepidation or anxiety for loss of their influence (unless one is well known or desired for a purpose or style). Keats may have had "it" in mind forming *Endymion*, to him, a beautiful allowable failure. "It" can be more democratic, not just subject to the "tyranny" of form, nor one-sided, literal or word by word in declension, but with liberty "found" in limits of form. Paradoxically "it" can promote transcendent processes (before reading Whitman's poems, Emerson knew this in his essays). When approached for fullness of experience of a good poem, "it," can manifest possessing the effect of music, notes in relation to one another, in relation to space and time, the space-time fabric plus god-like "simplification intensity" (Yeats, *A Vision*, phase 17) as in E=MC squared. With abstract art, what one perceives or gets from "it" is relative to what one brings to "it." Musical experience lies with the reader as with the piece.

The experience of the poem's speaker is generalized, specific to one then two people, then to a larger group, then students, as implied to an audience. Readers of the poem, may tie-up to opening observations, questions of the poem's two physics related ideas in a single thought/experience, may share duality of quantum physics principles which: 1. determine actual observation of quantum matter changes "it," 2. "broken in a throw of quantum dice" alludes to Einstein saying "God does not play dice with the universe" as being relative to law and the question of randomness in the universe and quantum mechanics. Implied is "proof of divine grand design" throughout the macro/micro (human parallel metaphor of inner/outer) universe. Among nature's mathematical laws, the firmament stars (and microscopic cellular structures) are God's bulwark for believers against ignorance and obstinate doubt of the divine.

It appears that the grand design part was not enough for Stephen Hawking to accept the divine part. Did his physical condition have some influence on his decision? Einstein appears to have gotten stuck mistakenly about certain over-arching aspects of quantum mechanics, according to the film *Einstein's Quantum Riddle*, (due to mere miscalculations of an equation?). He did not have a problem with the "God playing dice" thought/joke, was this because numbers proved "He" simply didn't play dice with the universe? Aspects of the quantum question are applied to relationships in the poem when assessing what is left of us after our dust returns and dreams have fled.

One need not understand all these things to appreciate poems. They may sound rhythmically intriguing, metrically with musical "numerical shapes" of word-sounds and lines to challenge, mysteriously delight. Poetic ideas may develop from particles relative to people and share some nature of entanglement. People take on time's numerical shapes, on larger but related scales to particles, implied by the "everything is connected" cliché, which both Einstein and Hawking were interested in proving. They conceptualized and failed beautifully to validate with equations, a "Theory of Everything," as the grand unifying principle of the known universe. Duality in quantum relationships, or entanglement, has bearing on an entity in how it effects and is effected by the other, regardless how far apart, or close, as "right there" in perpetuity. Even God for each person had to reduce the law to duality with a caveat. A poem's juxtapositions force the "unity" experience.

"Bell's Theorem" stipulates that particles once having interacted retain some strange link of connectivity no matter how arbitrarily far apart they get. Quantum Entanglement espouses that particles appear to communicate with each other across great distances. The symmetrical nature of the experience has to do with aspects of the universe studied, conjectured and theorized. Everything from shapes of bodies, planets, cells, etc., to the mind of God, seems born out by numerological aspects of the physical universe and time. This mystery may "add up," with specific details, to faith in an unseen greater beyond from this realm to ease the shock and awe of the unknown made known.

Questions arise, arriving at her neighbor's house, with no idea she is the neighbor's neighbor, from over a thousand miles away. More amazing details, after losing track of her again in 1974, involve marriage with her 22 years later in 1996. Susan's last name, always struck me as a combined German/English word, "aus," and "tell." For years that has been what I do with writing and when we married I felt that changing my name to hers would be more fitting, but we did not change names.

In one regard, later Susan tried to defeat me on many levels, while in earlier times she sought to encourage me in those same areas. She became an ultimate human relationship paradox, a true riddle only solved in death. She turned into my sphinx, and the answer to Susan's riddle, being my own man after her rejection, resulted in her slower yet just as real self-demise, done in by her own actions or lack of action, that played out against my best efforts to help her, without being over-bearing or covetous. She won in the end by beating herself, yet thanked me. I will wonder at length what could have changed the outcome.

The only solace, yet the greatest is, the "afterlife" (terrible expression) is far superior to this life, and the dream she appeared in after death, along with the dreams of Henry (dad) and Guy, prove it. This awareness leads to the idea of the true "double jeopardy" duality, the "second death" controlled by God is the true one to fear and we are in good hands there.

Quantum mechanics rings as true as being in the same class for four years of high school with Susan in Germany, because of WWII (the war that caused my birth in Würzburg, Germany) then scattered to different places in the United States, bumping into each other at White Sands, that strange missile base in New Mexico, near the atom bomb test site, (that helped end world war by threatening the whole world) then losing track of each other again only to marry years later ...entanglement indeed!

"Years later... late again" ...connotations not direct meaning, a feeling more than meaning, yet a truth to tell that infers her last name. These are devises that Shakespeare used and one would be hard pressed to glean a literal meaning from his Sonnets. There are veiled references, allusions, poetic tricks of tongue, compressed time, many openings for conjecture and also personal experience with aesthetic values, qualities, letting the form play into the experience. These aspects make it poetry not essay writing (where the two can and should blend from time to time as they do here). Essays strive for literal meaning qualities and can prove to be manifestos of parsing, poetry is more like a bird one needs to set free to more fully feel experience, hopefully even relish liberty taking flight from its cage of words, in an ironic paradox, to escape when caught (change when seen like photons).

"Remotely sworn" is an allusion to the explorations of quantum physicists into what is termed "Remote Viewing." If one looks up remote, one finds "remote controls" or "far away," viewing looked up finds "observing" or "looking at." If Remote Viewing is searched for, a psychic exercise is found that some physicists have experimented on with the C.I.A. ...the point is literal meaning does not automatically usher in the deepest experience with the best poetry, though it can help lay groundwork necessary for a transcendent experience.

A good read of good poetry achieves that thing referred to as reading between the lines, or what is not there, as with what is on the line and how words progress through the body of the poem. The last two lines are ending couplets in what developed as an adapted 3 sonnet "epiphany crown." The three part poem came from a dream series, dreams arriving in a thematic returning or haunting way. How dreams inspired other poems relates to how the first *Haunted Generation* poem occurred after a "mother conflict dream" Dr. Freud would have enjoyed interpreting. Though imagination seemed to play a larger part in the longer *Haunted Generation 2* than in the first poem of that name, a lot came from dream transcription of what happened in both. Form variations turn the three ending couplets into a coda where interpretations are not just for Dr. Freud.

The risk challenge of allusions brought another layer of imagination to the poems. The courage to form the poem is one purpose of enlightenment, as well as stimulation to read and risk open-minded non-judgmental, unconditional positive regard. Negative Capability, ironically named, is essential for this and writing like a true "quatrain meta-physicist" can at times recall Nostradamus.

An exploding supernova of poetry, Walt Whitman adorns the "Kosmos" as he calls it, with his own "silver face" on our poetic language. This silver image of Lincoln is in "When Lilacs Last in the Dooryard Bloomed" (pt. XVI. 197). Dr. Harold Bloom considers it the greatest single poem to date in any language in the Western Hemisphere (A/I p. 237). Whitman's "Lilacs" is the conversation of the "Oversoul's" intimate human song in its true sublime eloquent splendor. Yet Walt was slighted by perhaps the greatest political tactician of modern poetry, W. B. Yeats, in the cosmic, at turns veiled-fascistic, systematically structured judgment of his book, *A Vision*. Dr. Bloom in 2011's *The Anatomy of Influence* (p. 237) points out Yeats' compact judgment on the "Will," of Walt's entirety, voice/persona, as lost in the "Phase 6" paradigm of *A Vision*, where the "soul's free will suffers" another "A. I." –"Artificial Individuality." Here Yeats underestimates Walt's tallied up half-formed consciousness as having "created an Image of vague, half-civilized man, all his thought and impulse a product of democratic bonhomie."

I wonder what the AI of "Alexa" would portend from Yeats' neatly categorized lapsed "one-shot" "judgment," in accordance with an Amazon "Echo's one-shot" (*Wired* p. 63) "oracular answer?" As of yet "Alexa" cannot write a conscious haiku, much less a quatrain though it could probably beat Bobby Fischer at chess, one move at a time? Yeats may have used a relevant word, "democratic," that has something of a universal aspect appealing to the hope of humanity, in relation to Walt's transcendental "Kosmos."

This leads back to the touchstone dream series that continues: about a month after death, Susan's appearance, perfect in her glory, yet unobtrusively, gently, kindly with her utmost beauty's countenance of unconditional love, dutifully standing by a counter of what now seemed to be a "Kosmic" library, in a sublime nature setting, wearing a form fitting sleeveless warm black dress, intricate designs on the torso woven of geometric "curvism's symbolic truthmanship," emerging in chiaroscuro subtlety from the close-up background of smooth flat fabric, more futurist than Moorish patterns but a design subsuming both ideals. Her refined form, more real than her disease ravaged body or William Blake's sublime, rested in resurrected perfection's contentment. Her direct gaze as I slowly zoomed in on her face, perfect form and bettered Mona Lisa smile, stood in service before a fine solid narrow home bookcase, the top of which could not be seen, as if ever rising. Packed with books on each shelf, spines together, a multitude of color and design fragments, the patchwork mosaic seemed so abstract at first as to be unrecognizable as books, like a symbolic web-mystery of life. On further reflection, the shapes on her black dress were elegant horizontal long curved dual tipped "spearheads" like Lin's *Flight* shapes against the sky, in exquisite Flemish jewel colors emerging out of & back into a perfect chiaroscuro background tapestry, which is where the dream ended. Just as Walt's "Lilacs" were written for Lincoln, it's metaphysical thrust, intonations and implications seemed to also be true for Susan, Guy, Janice, you or me. I followed a reading of "Lilacs" in the gray solitude of an early April Saturday morning to write an ending quatrain for Walt, Susan, Guy and us:

> Between the lines' material, chasing the moon
> his Kosmos calls for an orbital lilac tree,
> its taproot tallying the orbs of destiny
> as I lie in glowing fields, dream up his night's tune.

To be courageous one confronts fears and lies. There is a saying that good fiction is a lie that tells the truth. When good poetry does this it does so to reach a higher truth than the literal words. There is a certain entanglement on the quantum level of words for dreams and experiences that have a haunting quality. Imagine a quantum physicist approaching the Bible's *Book of Daniel* with a certain clinging quality of dreams found there. They can renew ones spirit and wonder in order to overcome fear of being misunderstood. That process can exert a strong influence to anxiously read and write from, to find if ones words can prove worthy of the love it took to achieve them through fields of dreams.

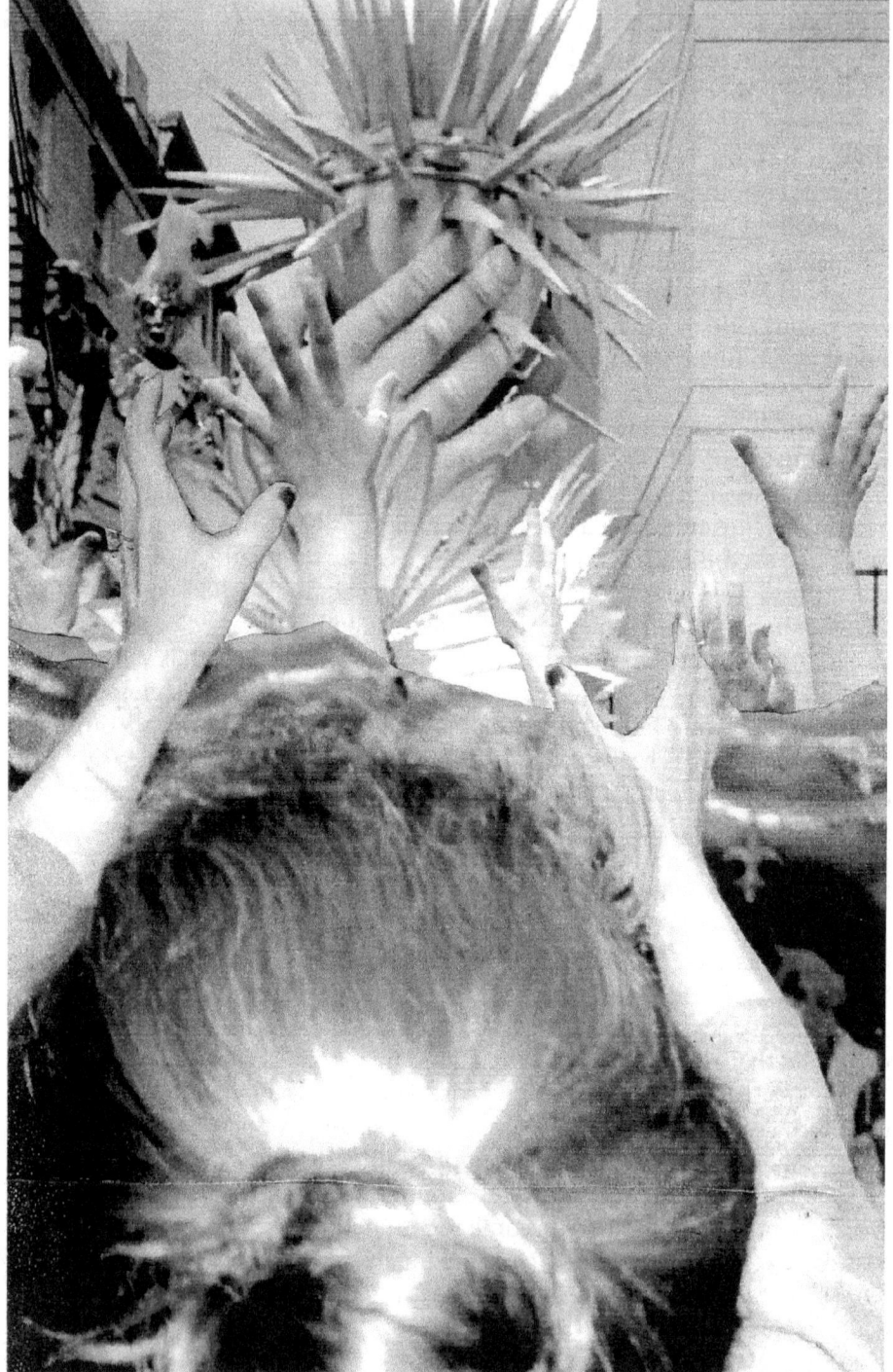

Appendix 2

Forming the Three Volumes

Shakespeare's Wake, volume one of a tribute to *Shakespeare's Sonnets*, was first planned to have 22 crowns and does with a twist: 21 with 7 sonnets (with variations on crown form), a 3 sonnet epiphany "crown-et," and 4 sonnets making 154 with allusions throughout from the 154 in Shakespeare's collection. There are 10 "transition" sonnets (not numbered for allusions) as intros and exits, all totaling 164 sonnets.

Volume two, *Recycling the Circle*, with 3 crowns, 1 epiphany crown and 58 sonnets (with variations) has 82. Volume three, *Romance Languages*, with a garland and crown, has 54 sonnets, for 300 in the trilogy.

The volumes contain tragedies, comedies, myth, some pieces include blends of romance, history and comedy like compressed inner "play-let shake-scenes" and heroic sonnet forms seeking to express the obvious and the indescribable as unified elevated experience. In this way a rose is never just a rose. The plan for three separate books with individual covers may serve volume distinctions better for some readers.

The last revision process planned Shakespeare sonnet allusions for each line, with each alluded to sonnet number beside titles or numbers in the volumes. Allusion numbers for the volumes 2 & 3 seem more erratic due to sequence changes as the volumes developed. The original number scheme for allusions still tended to work out even after revised sonnet position changes. Two 16 sonnet "dual redouble'" forms were dropped. Here is some revealing rigor examined.

The dual redouble' is my extension of the form with an "index" sonnet at each end, sonnet 1 and 16, instead of having just one index sonnet at the beginning or end of the regular 15 sonnet redouble' form. The eliminations changed a predetermined sequence of how sonnet allusions would come from Shakespeare's numbered sonnets in a direct count for each of mine, as in a "same numbered" sequence. Removing the first redouble' from volume one and the second from volume two, improved the end result when keeping the three best sonnets of the first redouble' and spreading them out in volume two, while reducing the other redouble' to a 7 sonnet crown and moving it to the epilogue of volume one, with Coverdale psalm allusions (as Shakespeare used in places) added & noted in each line.

This led to Coverdale allusions as well as sonnet allusions in 3 crowns. The sonnet allusions were not to be used more than once in each of the separate volumes but in volumes two and three a few repetitive sonnet allusion numbers occurred. The reasons for repeating the numbers had to do with changes like the earlier ones described, altering the predetermined numerical arrangement and volume placement, not merely due to random choice or similar thematic content. I lost track of how vol. 2 allusions began with #66 but it probably had to do with changes in the opening section line up. The Shakespeare sonnet number ordering for allusions in volume two felt at times like mixing watercolors, tuning a guitar or consulting the *I-Ching* with yarrow sticks found in the Bollingen translation with Carl Jung's "Synchronicity Foreward," but I did want to approach in numerically and not thematically which added an element of mystery.

The 3 volume single collection seemed to develop its own kind of "artificial Shakespeare intelligence" due to more considerations than merely an allusion scheme after long periods of placement changes and revision. Though intuitive adjustments in volume one's sonnet order and how Shakespeare's 1-154 allusion sonnets lined up to the epilogue changed after revisions, how vol. 1's selection placements led to vol. 2 and vol. 3 may have mystified C. G. Jung more than Joseph Campbell. The allusion process to not use a word or phrase more than once or more times than had been used by Shakespeare in a given sonnet (#42 has 7 "love" root word uses and #40 has 10!). Not over using allusions also extended to Coverdale psalms. Some later revisions (as in "Supernatural Bridge," "A Wandering Bark's Bliss," "Stephen Hawking's Mythology of Everything," "ASAP: Age of the Second Adam's Paradigm" and the transition sonnets) did not work well into the systematic allusion usage for each line without completely rewriting the poems and so were left unchanged.

The allusion sequence for volume three did not stem from how volume two developed but extended the pattern of a group of nine non- consecutive Shakespeare sonnet numbers listed in a row by author Gerald Massey in the 1888 book, *The Secret Drama of Shakespeare's Sonnets Unfolded* (p. 205 - 210). The narrative sequence involves different characters in what appears as a kind of operatic relationship struggle. Massey explains at length the narrative involving Shakespeare "friends" with clarifying detail fit for a courtroom drama, almost as if he had known the characters personally! Volume three, *Romance Languages*, is a romantic comedy in relation to the other two volumes. The first vol. deals with romance in the beginning section that ties into the Orpheus myth before the epilogue that blends everything from visionary dream epiphany to modern gothic horror, historical, dramatic, psychological and mythical/alchemical sequences). Comedic relief like pixie dust is generously sprinkled through various parts of the trilogy aided and abetted by all the rhyming and no blank verse. Even Shakespeare deviated from strict use of iambic pentameter from first to last syllable at times and I tried to be faithfully aware of the metrical sound of lines throughout even when variations were used.

As the essay conclusions reached the "operatic essence" of the Bard's *Sonnets* before discovering Gerald Massey's "unfolding" concept, it was amusing and bracing to find Massey's similar reading. From Massey's nearly absurd to clairvoyant-like detective work, his determination helped spur on the arduous task of rewriting to include, as a more challenging tribute, a numbered pattern of Shakespeare sonnet allusions (that would "puzzle through" each line) for the three volumes' selected sonnets. The turn the volumes took after allusions were set up resulted in very challenging, often puzzling results, but never failed to intrigue, amaze and amuse. (Turn to the last four sonnets in his series, listen for the humor that circulates there and try to imagine what that may have sounded like to the clever English dry witted ears of his readers at that time. The Bard exhibited all the hallmarks of elevated comedy there just as in his plays, perhaps even more concentrated in the sonnets.)

The allusion-sonnet order for volume 3, repeated in an extending cyclical pattern, Massey's narrative sequence of nine sonnets that were according to him (like opera) set to specific music (p. 210), that of Autolycus's music to *Two Maids Wooing a Man*. The nine sonnets he listed in a specific order (144, 33, 34, 35, 41, 42, 133, 134, 40) and a sample of his comments, are referred to and examined at the end of the essay *Shakespeare's Operatic Crown*.

The deaths of friends, Guy Charleville followed by Susan Austell less than a month later, spurred on a series of dreams, inquires, new poems, revisions of old poems and an essay resulting in a 4th volume, *Radio Waves for the Blind*, and a 5th that condensed the *quadrilogy* into a volume of 44 essential sonnets, prints & all essays.

Appendix 3
Shakespeare's Operatic Crown: a Confessional Secular Psalm-Mirror Cycle?

There are 154 poems in *Shakespeare's Sonnets* and 150 Psalms in the English Bible. The Sonnets may be read owing as much to form and quatrain development as content to achieve psalm-like epiphanies in an English Catholic-minded reinvented crown cycle. This essay strives for an unpopular analysis by certain upper echelon critics, in favor of what my research discoveries illuminate. Daniel Swift in his recent book *Shakespeare's Common Prayers* (p. 59) refers to a "gap," that points to a "history of exclusion," that "critical attention to the apparent religiosity of Shakespeare's plays has always left out the Book of Common Prayer a curiously forgotten work, overlooked even by those who might be expected to know it." This essay aims at a similar idea for the Sonnets in relation to the Psalms and other biblical works.

The formal sonnet elements lend a ceremonial sacramental complexity to secular-sacred continuums in William Shakespeare's sonnet arrangements. These "continuums" involve various unnamed fictionalized and personal relationships with friends, enemies, implied family members, society figures, nature, time and God. The book's dedication is to a friend or patron, one may assume a disguised friend due to the personal content of the Sonnets dispersed like little chapters or scenes of an anonymous emotional journey that spans sections of the sonnet-speaker's life with quasi and overt operatic intonations. This uncertainty spreads intentionally through the entire series following the dedication.

The Yale Shakespeare, 1923 editor of *Shakespeare's Sonnets*, Edward Bliss Reed, in his well noted appendices generalizes: "no part of Shakespeare's work arouses more interest or greater critical discussion... which has unfortunately arrived at no sure conclusions." He then groups the "sonnet collection problems" into three categories: "historical, literary and autobiographical." The historical problems involve identities and "events hinted at." Two literary problems are: when written and in what order placed for print. For "most disputed problem," the autobiographical, he cites a range of scholarly view points from "conventional themes and treatments" with "debates of eye and heart (in blazoning pen)" to "punning amusement and personal confession" (p. 92-5).

Many conjectures and assumptions have been made about who specific characters are in what would amount to an interior emotional, veiled character play spanning years. My contention is that it does not matter who the particular characters are, the internal narrative is universal to human nature as revealed in its context of unfolding aspects. More than vaguely a "game of courtiers" as Stephen Greenblatt once put it (p. 234), Shakespeare was too clever for that to be the main objective of the Sonnets.

In the context of his times and accomplishments of the age, one would consider highly noted literary events and what part of an event would be most influential and relative to understanding the development of the Sonnets. Clare Asquith (p. 21) refers to Sir Philip Sidney as "the most admired poet of the age" and his 1595 influential book *Defense of Poetry*, that explains his theory of "shadowed language" alluding to "mysterious deeper meanings" or " hidden matters," as bearing the "essence of good writing." But perhaps the most specific overwhelming achievement can be nothing less than the English translated *Book of Psalms*. The *Geneva Bible* of 1560, appearing more than 20 years after the Coverdale translation, used Coverdale as a source with certain corrections. The *Geneva's* first to number verses with extensive margin notes made it the most widely used during Shakespeare's time until the *King James Version* of 1611, which remained very close to the *Geneva Bible* in places like the metrical *Book of Psalms* (Bobrick p. 175). In the *Geneva Bible* one can see the narrative thread of King David's experiences being parsed throughout in the notes accompanying the text. One may also see the possible origins of Shakespearean mysticism in lines like Psalm 81:7, "...I delivered thee and answered thee in the secret of the thunder."

Since the Psalms were the grandest sequence of song/poems imaginable, various English translations were widespread and undertaken by translators from diverse backgrounds such as nobility, pious landowners, Catholic priests and reformers, scholars including Coverdale, King James I and Queen Elizabeth, Elizabethan sonneteers such as Sir Philip Sidney (Hotson p. 279) and his sister the Countess of Pembroke, who completed a collection   of translated psalms from what Sidney left incomplete in death at 32. The Psalms were considered the work of the shepherd/king David, some of which he supposedly composed on harp while watching over his flock. Elizabethan music was composed for many of these new translations to be sung (including all Coverdales's to the present) and "were closely linked... with lyrics called sonnets" (p. 279).

Aspects of King David's character were studied and absorbed from the narrative tales involving friends, family, loved ones, historical and social figures as well as enemies. Some of David's obvious relationships involved his friend Jonathan (whose friendship he referred to as better than a woman's love), King Saul (who loved David's music and tried to kill him), Bathsheba (who he coveted and claimed) and her husband the honorable soldier Uriah (who David sent into battle to be killed), as well as David's son Absalom (who tried to kill David and was killed himself) and others, not to leave out God, who considered David "a man after the Lord's own heart" (1 Sam. 13:14). Except for the Lord and David, none of these figures were named in the Psalms. No one is named in the Sonnets either except the puns on "Will" with oblique or veiled allusions to familiar ones and the Lord in places.

70

Shakespeare's devotion to the biblical text is shown in the extreme formal ordering of his sonnet elements and arrangements (even though imperfect like the human) and the highly respectable ebb and flow of closeness/distance he expresses to and for the "Holy of Holies." When his Sonnets were finally arranged and published there were deeper motives at work than romantic stories involving carnal emotional relationships. This too is seen in light of the happy "eternity promised" in the dedication, not for the mere sake of a pompous "parlor game among fanciful nobles." Yet the grand sequence is humbly dedicated to Mr. W. H. in a way as "fanfare for the common man" (even if a nobleman) which like the biblical Psalms can represent a multiplicity of emotional transcendent experience any mature human may relate to regardless of social standing. Shakespeare wrote during times of life and death struggle for how print on a page was accepted by law and the public. Bible translation was transforming English society in terms of monarchy demands (Asquith p. 23-24). Shakespeare, like a secret Catholic (Schneible), was careful about what and how he wrote which included plays and poems.

In the Psalms there is only the contemporary name David occurring in 6 Psalms, obliquely, perhaps in the third person or as mentioned by the Lord or scribes. A few Sonnets, 135 and 136 use "will" as in authorial punning for humor and insight, this paradoxically shows "Will's" self-effacing humility.

Professor Harold Bloom implies, had Shakespeare only written the Sonnets, the series would rank among the finest poems in world literary achievement (A. I. p. 91). When reading the Sonnets for psalm-like qualities, notes of irony sustain through Professor Bloom's remarks: "We all want to find him in the Sonnets, but he is too cunning for us, and you have to be the Devil himself to find Shakespeare there (G. p. 25)." One may suppose this is Dr. Bloom's Freudian Gnostic perspective, considering various critical interpretations of the Sonnets from Francis Meres (classically romantic) through Oscar Wilde (homoeroticism) and so on, saying more about the interpreter than author, which leaves Shakespeare's mysterious implications intact, "circulated among private friends."

In Helen Vendler's book *The Art of Shakespeare's Sonnets* she discounts autobiographical, even Christian nature there and takes issue with essay-like readings for meaning analysis of the Sonnets, by critics like Stephen Booth (p. 13), in favor of pure aesthetic value, while she agrees Sonnet 116 is one of the finest. She spares readers copious metrical analysis, which she quips "would make another book" she feels "not competent to write" as others may like Booth (p. 11) but first offers apologetic wiggle-room: "total emersion in the Sonnets –that is to say, in Shakespeare's mind- is a mildly deranging experience to anyone, and I cannot hope, I suppose, to escape the obsessive features characterizing Shakespearean Sonnet criticism," as if pardoning herself at the outset for any possible arrogance (p. 1).

Dr. Stephen Greenblatt's view, "By keeping his poems at some remove from the actual, Shakespeare was able both to share them intimately... and to circulate them safely among readers," (p. 235) contributes to understanding their personal and potentially dangerous socio-religious political content. A variety of experts claim at length what was or was not essential creation and purpose of *Shakespeare's Sonnets*. Formal elements facilitate ranges of subtle emotion and multiple layers of meaning (Asquith p. 283). Sonnet 29 shows deep anguish, "myself almost despising" and transcendent exaltation, "sings hymns at heaven's gate."

Sonnet 116 takes off on the *Book of Common Prayer's* marriage vow, "Let me not to the marriage of true minds," recalling psalm-like structure in *New Testament, I Corinthians 13*, and informs, alludes to the list there, of what love is not. He moves into comedic conceit of the "unknown" value love has as guide for referred-to-ones in: "every wandering bark," "although his height be taken." Transcendent measure of love is ramped up as "not Time's fool." When brief, love can spark endurance "even to the edge of doom." Doubt resolves in a double negative paradoxical hymn-like vow's epiphany, that dares belief in these ideas as error: if wrong he never wrote "nor no man ever loved," which concludes his most profound succinct ode to love as an already highly acclaimed author.

In her book, *Shadowplay: The Hidden Beliefs and Coded Politics of William Shakespeare*, Clare Asquith delves into Sonnet 152's veiled politics: King James I's betrayal of Catholics and the sonnet speaker's patience with an oath of support which self-beguilingly acted as collusion with persecution (p. 285). In terms of "hidden belief" analysis, one could argue outside of the Psalms, the Sonnets are prime examples of early complex coded political and "Confessional Poetics" as a genre or Ars Poetica.

William Wordsworth's deduction of the Sonnets in his own sonnet, "Scorn not the Sonnet," reads: "with this key / Shakespeare unlocked his heart." The Sonnets were discreetly dedicated to Mr. W. H., who one might assume to be the "young man" first addressed in them. The dedication made by publisher Thomas Thorpe (T. T.) did not mean Shakespeare played no part in dedicating, or in the publication as an ordered series, he could have retained discreet background controls in1609. Professor Greenblatt understands the sonnet "game of love" Shakespeare carefully plays "could lead to the Tower and the scaffold" (p. 234). He presents a possibility that the Sonnets were commissioned and started because he needed money when plague caused theaters to be closed, a time (1592) when he appeared to be transitioning from "successful playwright to cultivated poet" (p. 240-1). Francis Meres in his 1598 book *Wits Treasury,* praised his popular "sugared sonnets among his private friends" and esteemed Shakespeare's "mellifluous honey tongue" with Ovid's "sweet witty soul."

Seeking patronage he wrote *Venus and Adonis* and *The Rape of Lucrece* with dedications to late-teen unmarried Earl of Southampton. Dr. Greenblatt deduces that if the first 126 sonnets "were written to the same person... they sketch a relationship unfolding... over years. Admiration ripens into adoration; periods of joyful intimacy are followed by absence and desperate longing..." (p. 246).

Thorpe's dedication, "To The Onlie Begetter" was like a spin on the   Catholic *Apostle's Creed* phrase "only begotten son." The allusion is identified by Yale editor Edward Bliss Reed in his *Notes* section of the 1923 *Shakespeare's Sonnets* facsimile (p. 78) of *The Yale Shakespeare*. Yale published the works of Shakespeare as a same-sized volume set, including the Sonnets. A volume of *Venus and Adonis, Lucrece and the Minor Poems* edited by Albert Feuillerat has extensive notes and   appendices. The volume contains *The Passionate Pilgrim* of 1599: 2 poems in two sections, the first contains Shakespeare Sonnets 138 and 144 and two sonnets from the play *Love's Labors Lost*. The   second section, *Sonnets to Sundry Notes of Music*, contains a fifth verse poem like a song   not a sonnet from *Love's Labors Lost* IV. iii: 101-120. It is not consistent with sonnet form and a character in the play, Dumaine, refers to it as an ode. This bolsters my understanding of the musical nature of *Shakespeare's Sonnets* in which most recent critical experts seem to gloss over along with the strength of psalm allusions.

Dr. Reed's notes on Sonnet 112. 10, 11. (p. 87): "that my adder's sense to critic and to flatterer stopped are" point to the use of "deaf adder" snake imagery as perhaps oblique allusion to Psalm 58 lines 4 & 5, while using an exact *Coverdale Psalter* quotation: "Even like the deaf adder, that stoppeth her ears; Which refuseth to hear the voice of the charmer, charm   he never so wisely." Dr. Stephan Booth's notes (also Yale published) on Sonnet 112's "deaf adder" allusion, uses the *Geneva Bible* quotation rather than Coverdale. He follows with an ironic comment (p. 364): "(Note the expression was traditionally for those who refused to hear truth.)" Dr. Booth's ironic "not hearing truth" due to omissions are noticed   by "psalm" and "Coverdale" missing from his index. 50 biblical allusions are indexed at "Bible," 3 psalms are noted, not Psalm 58, referred to in his commentary on Sonnet 112. Dr. Booth makes no mention of the 4 oblique Psalm 17 allusions (I point out later) in Sonnet 17 which also contains the image of "antique song."

The Creed allusion suggests that the "blessing" to Mr. W. H. was on a different level than callow youth, rival poet or rival lover, more like one whose relationship "unfolded over years," resolving in the "sweet nothings" of the last two Sonnets' love myth with a cheeky "all's well that ends well" ending of laughs & smiles to draw a happy curtain on the "154 Sonnets cycle." Love's happy spiritual enterprise is conveyed by the dedication's hope: "All Happiness and that Eternitie Promised by Our Ever-Living Poet," to cover religious and mythical ideals (like proverbial parables) in happiness pursuits of the ever interestingly flawed yet transcendent human. A similar joyous ending exclaims from the final Psalms 149 and 150. Participants are involved with dancing, singing, playing musical instruments while exhorted to make "new" songs of praise to the Lord, conveying an endless expression of redemption praising love as a clear universal ideal (as done by W. S.).

From the first Sonnet's first line to last Sonnet's last, the dedication- fulfilling cycle achieves exponential reinvention effects of an extended   crown of sonnets. The first line's universal "we" in "we desire increase" wants the same as plural God, *Genesis* 1:26, who also commands "Increase and multiply" (...new songs and souls? Yes.).   An allegorical tease, "little love-god," of the last Sonnet's first line, displays wit for the "fairest creatures" from the first Sonnet, as receiver of that promised "Eternitie" the "alpha and omega" of this Sonnet series -first line to last: "From fairest creatures we desire increase" "Love's fire heats water, water cools not love." Enlightenment, shown in Shakespeare's   psychological humorous myth development of desire, seeks to spur (perhaps the dedicatee) on to fulfill pleasant biblical tasks of providing "increase."

Marchette Chute in her charming book, *Shakespeare of London*, quotes Thomas Thorpe's formal dedication: "To the Right Honorable, William, Earl of Pembroke... etc.," that goes on for ten more lines before Thorpe signs, "Your Lordship's humble devoted T. T." Chute's point is Thorpe's dedication of the Sonnets to Mr. W. H. could not have been for a nobleman, only a commoner (p. 343); no mention of Psalms is given other than of King James I, a published author, translating "some of the Psalms," who had written "a study of the *Apocalypse*," "a treatise on demonology," while "having produced a great many poems" and "a book of advice to poets" (p. 253-4). Benson Bobrick (p. 267) concludes that the literary King James I was so weak in other areas of rule that after his death, it resulted in the English civil war, a culmination of conflict between the Crown, Catholics and anti-papist/reformers such as the Puritans.

Wait for more irony. Chute relates "unicorn tales" brought to London from America: "Unicorns were mentioned even in the Bible and it was well known that the horn of the animal, pulverized and boiled in wine, made an excellent mouthwash" (p. 62). This was Chute's extent of biblical allusion commentary, amusing but zilch when it came to Psalm allusions found in Shakespeare's writing. The irony is if she had looked in the Bible for where unicorns are "seen" she could have found Psalm 29 (& 92) where Coverdale's English translated Psalter was set to be sung in church with this pair of lines: "He maketh them also to skip like a calf; / Libanus and Sirion, like a young unicorn."

Close reading reveals key words and conceptual phrases from Myles Coverdale's metrical English Psalms permeate (through direct or oblique allusion) overall structure of the Sonnet series with several Sonnets having same-numbered Psalm allusions. The Sonnets work like a strange ironic mirror, Shakespeare's personal mirror of *Psalms*, *Proverbs*, *The Song of Solomon*, *I Corinthians 13*, etc., all together, no named characters, yet at times individuals (i.e. young man, rival poet, dark lady, etc.) are consecutively implied. This makes the Sonnet cycle a currently alive, perpetual veiled narrative gift, like Shakespeare's secular "psalm-ets" of love (Hotson p. 271-281).

Dr. Leslie Hotson saw allusions in parallel numbered Sonnet and Psalm 107 (with Sonnet 107's Armada crisis background) and 124 (alluding to an assassination plot) (p. 270). Other Sonnets with same-numbered Psalm allusions (6, 32, 51, 102) for Hotson proved Shakespeare's "canonical order of the Sonnets" (p. 280). Sonnet/Psalm allusions in Hotson's notes (p. 281) come from the *Coverdale Psalter* translation (1535) updated later for *The Book of Common Prayer* through Shakespeare's day when "Psalm-singing parishioners included theatre-goers" (p. 272). These Psalms remained in *The Book of Common Prayer* among Catholics and church reformers alike to current times. Hotson also cites Richard Noble's writing, *Shakespeare's Biblical Knowledge* (1935), which indicates there are "some 150 Psalm references from the plays" (p. 272) (same number coincidentally, as Psalms in the Bible).

Hotson points out where in Psalm 6 and Sonnet 6 loss of "beauty" sets tone and image. Then in Psalm and Sonnet 32, image of "my bones" in death sets the tone. Psalm and Sonnet 102 share mournful sound images: a sparrow in the Psalm and Philomel singing in the Sonnet (p. 281). This prompted a search for allusions from other Psalms in corresponding numbered Sonnets. Sonnet 1's first line, mentioned earlier, "From fairest creatures we desire increase" alludes to perhaps the fairest creatures of all, Adam and Eve, and the "increase and multiply" directive. It also obliquely alludes to the image in Psalm 1: "like a tree planted by the water-side that will bring forth his fruit in due season. / His leaf also shall   not wither." These allusions add universal implications to the Sonnet.

Sonnets 29, 43 and 116 contain allusions to corresponding numbered Psalms, though some allusions are more oblique than overt. Sonnet 29's theme contends with rising above self-dejection in remembrance of transcendent love that nothing can negate. It takes us from depths of self-loathing, "almost despising," to "sweet love rememb'red" compared to upward flight, as in a new day, away from moody earthbound morass, to "sing hymns at heaven's gate," where he would "scorn to change" his "state with kings."

The subtext of Psalm 29 recalls glorious ways the Lord interacts with nature, lands and people, where the Lord is above terrors of flood and remains "a King forever." In the last lines, "the Lord shall give strength onto his people" and "the blessings of peace" are alluded to in Sonnet 29 by what "such wealth brings."

Sonnet 43's allusion to Psalm 43's: "O send out thy light and thy truth, that they may lead me," is made as the speaker states his "eyes" in dream "are bright in dark directed" "with thy much clearer light" where his "eyes be blessed made," fitting the Psalm's tonal allusion, "that I may go unto the altar of God... the God of my joy and gladness." Redemptive implications are the same in both. The Psalm asks for defense of "my cause against the ungodly people" and for deliverance "from the deceitful and wicked man" while the Sonnet begins with colloquial comedic slang, "when most I wink," as the speaker refers to seeing best in dreams because with awake eyes: "all the day they view things unrespected," which mirrors the Psalm's perception of injustice.

In Psalm 116, "I will pay my vows" is found twice, first followed with "now in the presence of all his people" and a few passages later, "in the sight of all his people," for a chorus effect. Psalm 116's theme is how the Lord reveals his love through deliverance. Preservation is offered to "the simple" when one in misery hastily exclaims, "All men are liars," yet is heard by the Lord with "the cup of salvation." Remembrance of what the Lord has done for him compels the speaker's devotion to pledge vows of service. Service is oppositely implied by the sonnet speaker's ending, if wrong he "never writ, nor no man ever loved." The overall sense of Sonnet 116 resolves like a series of vows that moves into a sworn "negative" oath at the end.

Religious connotations in Sonnet 29 extend like a "Big Bang" of enlightenment from the compact sonnet form. Shakespeare's crown like extensions and Psalm-mirroring evokes strength and weakness characterizing human condition. Beaut is in the mind's ear, beheld by close readers, loved ones recognizing themselves, interchangeable, revealing extended goals of love, for others as for oneself.

In response to those only seeing "thinness of or lack of pervasive Psalm-mirroring" in the Sonnets, I compared Coverdale's (and the *Geneva*) Psalm 17 to Sonnet 17 that use key words like "heaven." The allusions there, quoting Sonnet then Psalm are: "hides your life / hide me under; beauty of your eyes / apple of an eye; men of less truth than tongue / men, I say, and from the evil world; some child of yours / They have children."

Sonnet 17 also has a good lead-in for a few concluding epiphanies. The poet refers to his "papers" being "scorned" generally and by what is specifically embodied in 17, his inability to accurately describe beauty attributes of the loved one addressed. He gives that future critics would say "this poet lies" with the "stretch`ed miter of an antique song" plying a metrical (and "crown" metaphor?) idea in the line which also lends song- like echo (Help me, Helen Vendler (p. 116) who copies miter as meter as if to correct spelling) to the ending couplet's singing rhyme of time / rime.

Coverdale's Psalms, praised for musicality are used in *Handel's Messiah* and retain their place in the English Psalter of churches throughout England with tweaked adjustments over the years for being sung or read like an English cross-denominational Bible text.

In Shakespeare's play, *Love's Labor's Lost*, Act IV, Scene III, line 157 reads, "Tush, none but minstrels like of sonneting!" To read his Sonnets more deeply one needs to be aware of historical context, family life and socialization in line with his vast literary talents. Music was an important part of his life influenced by religious practice and as an actor/playwright. His Sonnets, like 29, 43 and 116 can be sung as melodiously as any Coverdale Psalm adjusted over the years.

With the concept of Carl Jung's universal pool of the unconscious mind, one could argue that even modern day English pop songs like the Beatles' "Let it Be" (a phrase that came to Sir Paul McCartney in a dream, spoken to him for consolation by his departed mother, as he said after singing it, on James Cordon's *Late Late Show*, "Carpool Karaoke" in Liverpool, June 16, 2018 on the CBS Network) and "Eleanor Rigby," stem from English Psalter tradition, which *Shakespeare's Sonnets* seem to mirror at times and take part in its crowning achievements (as great hymns do like English clergyman John Newton's 1773 "Amazing Grace," sung by President Barak Obama at a memorial service for slain Black Charleston, South Carolina church members).

With this Sonnet cycle Shakespeare reinvented the crown of sonnets by doing away with repetitive last line/first line motifs in favor of conceptual development forms that vary from the traditional crown of seven sonnets. Some scholars like Sir Edmund Chambers and Northrop Frye (Hotson p. 269) see the first 126 as being in Shakespeare's chronological sequence with the following Sonnets possibly arranged by the first publisher (T. T.). Both 126 and 154 are divided evenly by 7. The 154 Sonnets contain 22 crown's worth of sonnets, where the number is closest to the 150 Psalms.

While contemplating scholarly commentary in regard to certain seemingly obvious analytical points pertaining to *Shakespeare's Sonnets*, I glanced at the Jan. 1, 2018 cartoon cover of *The New Yorker* magazine dominated by a huge oblivious grey elephant in a large sketchy living room, standing between a silently seated vexed looking older couple deep in their own annoyed thoughts. The title is: "Cramped" and comes from the hand of cartoonist George Booth, in my imagination somehow related to that heavy lifter of Sonnet commentary, Stephen Booth, whose massive commentary (nearly 450 pgs.) is the "elephant in the room" and needs addressing in terms of my "big picture" understanding of *Shakespeare's Sonnets* as a deliberate operatic epic with peaks, valleys, variations "doing the police in different voices," held together by circular language, codes, allusions, form and metrics.

Sonnet 8 seems to be the closest Dr. Booth gets to the musicality of the whole Sonnet enterprise, a bit ironically as the first line runs, "Music to hear, why hear'st thou music sadly?" In commentary on this (p. 144) he refers to the "serious logical inconsistency" of its "chiasmically balanced epithet and question" echoing exaggerations that then "analyze the inconsistency with inappropriately rigorous logic" through the descending lines of the quatrain (thick irony had here considering Booth's own devises, such is what award winning stuff like his immense book is made of!) he gets the coming "sexual overtones" and parses them handily all the way to the "concord" and "union" of sonnet matrimony. Then following two pages of commentary he lands on an oblique reference to a possible Shakespeare pun attempt used similarly in the play, *All's Well that Ends Well* III.ii.20-22, with a play on words "not, note," with "knot" as what a Renaissance reader may actually have heard!

This leads to his ironic oversight as a near aside to Webster's dictionary: "knot" somehow meaning "ornamental garden," as Booth finds in "...(John) Marston's play *Malcontent*, where Burbadge (theater proprietor, "The Money" buffoon (?) in the film: *Shakespeare in Love*) says (musical) additions introduced into the play are "only as your salad to your great feast, to entertain a little more time, and to abridge the not-received custom of music in our theatre (p. 146)." Here I will leave the elephant's ironically cramped room for wider spaces where arias may be heard in the open air!

The Sonnets accomplish a sublime expression of craft and personal/universal experience that was best achieved first by the ancient Greeks and "King David's" Psalms which were works known to be sung. David's name is in 6 Psalms. There are tribes and nations but no other contemporaries of David are named. Historical figures are mentioned: Moses, Aaron, Abraham, Isaac, Dathan, Abiram, Phinehas, Melchizedek, Joseph, Jesse and Jacob (mostly, over a dozen times). The only woman found mentioned is in Psalm 51's added intro statement of the 1560 *Geneva Bible* of Shakespeare's time; the Psalm's commentary states it is David's cry for mercy in fallen sinfulness after approached by the prophet Nathan revealing David's sin against and with Bathsheba.

Shakespeare's personal Sonnet "odyssey," like David's, is Homeric and mythic/anti-mythical but with no names though various sonnets sound like different character voices, even female at times, similar to his dramas. Gerald Massey in his 1888 book, *The Secret Drama of Shakespeare's Sonnets Unfolded,* after offering eloquent investigative evidence like a trial lawyer, points out characters Shakespeare knew and veiled in the Sonnets with their personal traits and dramatic motives. Massey presents a group of Sonnets:

144, 33, 34, 35, 41, 42, 133, 134, 40, in this explicated order (p. 205-10) and goes on to say:

"Elizabeth Vernon's jealousy of her lover the Earl of Southampton and her friend and cousin Lady Rich, is told in these nine sonnets, which are now for the first time put together: they go to Autolycus's tune of "Two Maids Wooing a Man." The first sonnet contains a soliloquy on the subject, a form employed more than once in the dramatic Sonnets. Then we have five Sonnets addressed to the Earl, and three to the lady of whom Elizabeth Vernon is jealous (Lady Rich) (p. 210-11)."

Autolycus, the ballad selling rogue in *The Winter's Tale*, 4.4.310-13, refers to a merry ballad which "...goes to the tune of 'Two Maids Wooing a Man:' here's scarce a maid westward but she sings it; tis in request, I can tell you." Massey seems to know the tune enough to capitalize on it in 1888. By 2017, Catherine Henze in her book *Robert Armin and Shakespeare's Performed Songs*, refers to the song among others also sung by Armin as Autolycus. She notes the lyrics but not the music came down to us (as Autolycus' other song melodies did) (p. 84). In 1599, Armin, also a writer (*Quips for Questions*) was hired as a musician/actor by Shakespeare for the Chamberlain's Men and took on the primary roll of the fool (p.1).

Considering Massey's sonnet list order, 33 with ambiguous heavy allegorical landscape imagery, "glorious morning," then spiritual allusions of "celestial face" and "heaven's sun," sounds like a more fitting soliloquy or overture than144. Line 11 of 33, plays loss off of the allegory in a climactic outburst: "But, out! alack! he was but one hour mine," on to end, "heaven's sun staineth." The list goes on fine through 134, then 144 would return to the allegorical images of 33 as a romantic struggle with "good & bad angels." Lastly, 40 bids for an overwhelming conflict resolution hope with "love" used 10 times!

Clare Asquith in her "Selection of Coded Terms" (p. 299) refers to 33 as alluding to Christ's passion and age of death and the age Shakespeare was when his son Hamnet died, which seems most fitting to bear the grandest allegorical and transcendent soliloquy weight of his Sonnet series.

Regarding the veiled sonnet characters named by Massey, it is compelling to see the Lady Penelope Rich saga Massey lays out, with Sir Philip Sidney's connection (p. 352-6), is also brought out in agreement but with more emphasis on Sidney, by Clare Asquith in 2005's *Shadowplay* (p. 151). Massey compiled such a thorough dossier on Lady Rich's beauty that perhaps even Cleopatra's beauty received less notice by Shakespeare. Massey argues at length that Lady Rich, the first love (though unrequited) of Sir Sidney, was the model for Shakespeare's later Dark Lady sonnets (after #126 and earlier) as well as being Sidney's "chiaroscuro" eyed inspiration for Stella (p. 356). Clare Asquith compiles a similarly weighty analysis of Sir Sidney being the linchpin model/influence for the character and voice of Hamlet from several aspects included in his books: *A Defense of Poesie*, *Arcadia* and his epic sonnet sequence *Astrophel and Stella*, as well as the facts and legendary points of interest pertaining to his English nobility and death at 32 by an infected thigh wound in a described indecisive/useless action (p. 147-52). Clare Asquith refers to *A Defense of Poetry* as: "...colloquial, graceful, at once casual and learnedly authoritative, in the witty tradition of Erasmus and Montaigne... a bastion of common sense, written in reply to a critic on the theatre... ." Lady Rich, according to Asquith, as "the beautiful and intelligent sister of Essex (who was beheaded for treason), an active member of his dissident circle," was one who "...may have been providing acceptable cover for poetry that was in fact political and religious" in aiding Catholics (p.149). Lady Asquith points out Sidney's writings as: "elaborately allegorical, (that) suggest a gradual disillusion with English Protestantism, and a growing sympathy with the plight of Catholicism" (p. 149).

Turning to Sir Sidney's "Petrarchan" sonnet sequence *Astrophel and Stella*, from which allusions may be seen in Hamlet's voice and divided character and in other plays like *Richard III*, the basic idea is found there for a monumental Shakespeare sonnet sequence. Parallels can be found in Sidney's lines: Sonnet 69.7, "Gone is the Winter of my miserie!" calls to mind Richard III's, "Now is the winter of our discontent." Hamlet's echo can be heard in Sidney's Sonnet 68.10: "Labour to kill in me this killing care" and Sonnet 69.14, "No kings be crown'd but they some covenants make."

Music allusions are found in *Astrophel and Stella*: Sonnet 68.6 on Stella: "With voice more fit to wed Amphion's lyre," for his Muse in Sonnet 70.3-6:

> She oft hath drunk my tears, now hopes to enjoy
>
> Nectar of mirth, since I love's cup do keep
>
> Sonnets be not bound Prentice to annoy;
>
> Trebles sing high, so well as basses deep;

Then 70.9-14 ends with:

> Come then, my Muse, shew thou height of delight
>
> In well raised notes; my pen, the best it may,
>
> Shall paint out joy, though in but black and white.
>
> Cease, eager Muse; peace, pen, for my sake stay,
>
> I give you here my hand for truth of this,
>
> Wise silence is best musicke unto blisse.

Having achieved the romantic equivalence of "rock star" status after death, Sir Sidney's ending verse here even calls to mind Hamlet's fitting epitaph: "The rest is silence" among his "flight of angels."

Without referring to or judging for or against named individuals, *Shakespeare's Sonnets* resonate universally and instrumentally "Catholic" in their structured confessional sounding concepts of emotional themes (variations of love and betrayal). They can be read as parody of grand literature, the English Bible or immense authorial authority gravely ironic in places. Perhaps no greater irony exists anywhere in English literature so sublimely framed, maintained and followed-through. The sequence could be said to work with the same inner mechanics as the "poem unlimited" Shakespeare conceptualized in *Hamlet*.

The lyrical structure based on the crown of sonnets form, makes the Sonnets with anonymous characters, potentially one of the greatest modern operas ever conceived had only someone like Mozart lived long enough to find them and compose with an English librettist, something along the combined lines of *Cosi Fan Tutte*, *The Marriage of Figaro*, *The Magic Flute*, *Don Giovanni*, and his *Requiem* of, by and for love.

Works Cited

Asquith, Clare. Shadowplay: The Hidden Beliefs and Coded Politics of William Shakespeare. New York, N. Y.: Public Affairs, 2005. Print.

Bloom, Harold. Genius: A Mosaic of One Hundred Exemplary Creative Minds. New York, N. Y.: Warner Books, 2002. Print.

Bloom, Harold. The Anatomy of Influence: Literature as a Way of Life. New Haven, Conn.: Yale UP, 2011. Print.

Bobrick, Benson. Wide as the Waters: The Story of the English Bible and the Revolution It Inspired. New York, N. Y.: Simon & Schuster, 2001. Print.

Booth, Stephen. –ed. Shakespeare's Sonnets. New Haven, Conn.: Yale UP, 1977. Print.

Chute, Marchette. Shakespeare of London. N. Y., N. Y.: E. P. Dutton Co., 1949. Print

Coverdale, Myles. Coverdale's Psalter. San Bernardino, CA: Walter Pub. 2016. Print.

Greenblatt, Stephen. Will in the World: How Shakespeare became Shakespeare. New York, N. Y.: W. W. Norton & Co., 2004. Print.

Henze, Catherine A. Robert Armin and Shakespeare's Performed Songs. N. Y., N. Y. Routledge, 2017. Print.

Hotson, Leslie. Mr. W. H. London: Rupert Hart-Davis, 1964. Print.

Massey, Gerald. The Secret Drama of Shakespeare's Sonnets Unfolded. London, Spottiswoode and Co., 1888. Print.

Reed, Edward Bliss. The Yale Shakespeare: Shakespeare's Sonnets. New Haven, Conn.: Yale UP, 1923. Print.

Schneible, Ann. Was Shakespeare a Secret Catholic? Rome, Italy: CAN/EWTN News, 2016. Web. 20 June, 2016.

Swift, Daniel. Shakespeare's Common Prayers. N. Y., N. Y.: Oxford UP, 2013. Print.

Vendler, Helen. The Art of Shakespeare's Sonnets. Cambridge: Harvard UP, 1999. Print.

Afterword

The 2016 essay on his Sonnets, in the appendix, marked the 400 year death anniversary of Shakespeare and caused reimagining this text as a more thorough tribute. Tulane University professor and Louisiana State Poet Laureate, Peter Cooley, hosted the Sonnet part of a month long series of anniversary events called "First Folio!" The 2016 elaborate production featured readings, recitals, plays, displays of period publications of plays, the Sonnets and an actual *First Folio* opened to *Hamlet* under a Plexiglas cube in Tulane's newly established Newcomb Art Museum.

My trilogy tribute idea with allusions emerged after the essay research. One volume combining the essay and the 3 separate volumes seemed a worthy tribute at 300 sonnets (a number advised 5 years earlier to round the contents down to, from approximately twice that, prior to the essay, by a poet/editor/teacher friend). Reading the essay one can see where my allusion idea came from and what motivations Shakespeare may have had in allusion usage considering the importance of English Bible translations. All Coverdale's translated 150 Psalms in *The Book of Psalms* are also in England's *Book of Common Prayer*.

Many scholars say Shakespeare's allusion choices spread personal, romantic, historical, allegorical, spiritual and philosophical enrichments throughout his work. A more recent young scholar, Daniel Swift in his 2013 Oxford University Press book, *Shakespeare's Common Prayers: The Book of Common Prayer and the Elizabethan Age*, for 280 plus pages examines how influential the BCP was on Shakespeare's life & work.

When referring to Sonnet 23 (p. 78) he states generally: "The sonnets are games of form and articulation: they are about what truth may be boxed in set speech. Here the truest speaker is an actor, straining for the words of his role." Soon (p. 79) Swift transitions to the Sonnet embodied in Romeo and Juliet's dialogue, "upon meeting" they "speak instantly of holiness" as if a direct embodiment of the prayer book's influence:

ROMEO: If I profane with my unworthiest hand

       This holy shrine, the gentler sin is this:

       My lips, two blushing pilgrims, ready stand

       To smooth that rough touch with a tender kiss.

JULIET: Good pilgrim, you do wrong your hand too much,

       Which mannerly devotion shows in this.

       For saints have hands that pilgrims' hands too touch,

       And palm to palm is holy palmers' kiss.

ROMEO: Have not saints lips, and holy palmers, too?

JULIET: Ay, pilgrim, lips that they must use in prayer.

ROMEO: O then, dear saint, let lips do what hands do:

       They pray; grant thou, lest faith turn to despair.

JULIET: Saints do not move, though grant for prayers' sake.

ROMEO: Then move not while my prayer's effect I take. (1.5.90-103)

An interesting relative passage is found in Harold Bloom's, *A Map of Misreading*, (p. 67) that refers to Milton's "power of religious phenomenology:"

"As a man, evidently he was Christian (of his own sect, a sect of one) but as poet he was a fierce Miltonist, and as much a son of himself as of God. If the Imagination, in poetry, speaks of itself, then it speaks of origins, of the archaic, of the primal, and above all of self-preservation." Next examining Vico's "magic formalism" used as a tool of the "self-defining function of imagination," Dr. Bloom refers to Auerbach's summary: "The aim of primitive imagination... is not liberty but... establishment of fixed limits, as a psychological and material protection against the chaos of the surrounding world." Thank you Dr. Bloom, several of these aspects mentioned in both passages resonate throughout *Shakespeare's Sonnets* as well as the general structure and purpose of this trilogy.

The formal high modern English with which Shakespeare was well acquainted to the point of being dramatically responsible for its vocabulary expansion through his writing, was based on a good grounding in the holy scriptures, mythology and readings throughout the liberal arts, in law as well as good grammar and Latin education. My own research over the years in a liberal arts education, masters degree in counseling, masters studies in art history, and creative writing as part of an MFA curriculum in poetry and independent studies in the English Bible, immersion in documentary films repeated regularly on cable's History Channel, YouTube videos and the PBS television network, have added to the development of comprehension skills that assisted in propelling me to achieve these poetic works and enlightened thoughts.

Though the title, *Shakespeare AI*, may be a misnomer, it is a catchy "iconcurchaic" one that may afford some stimulation to the poetic memory banks in order to purchase its license worth of parody as well as profundity. One of the bravest challenge pursuits was to include the allusions throughout the trilogy requiring a complete revision of the text. Because of the allusion process the work takes on an even more profound aspect of an "artificial Shakespeare intelligence" which is how the title transformation into *Shakespeare AI*, was justified. This title was lastly and strangely aided and abetted by a curious essay in *The Atlantic* magazine, "How the Enlightenment Ends: Philosophically, intellectually –in every way –human society is unprepared for the rise of artificial intelligence" by Dr. Henry A. Kissinger (*The Atlantic*, June 2018). The cover headline refers to it as: *AI and the End of Human History* (quite an opposite bookend to Dr. Harold Bloom's published concept of: *Shakespeare: the Invention of the Human!*) The title *Shakespeare's Wake*, chosen for volume one, came from one of Dr. Harold Bloom's descriptions of James Joyce's *Finnegans Wake (A. of I.*, p. 112). In the concluding poem, *ASAP*, (last sonnet written for this trilogy) some key words were also inspired by Dr. Bloom, from passages in his 1996 book on "The Gnosis of Angels,

Dreams, and Resurrection," *Omens of Millennium*. It is interesting to note that I had not read enough of the book for it to consciously influence the writing of the trilogy before its final poem. I was excited to find several correlations in our use of words and ideas while recently reading his book more deeply, I will return to it. A current version of the poem *ASAP* uses the words: "archon" and "Pleroma" from his splendorous book (p. 239-40).

The term "iconcurchaic" is my invention that is a tribute to the Parisian poet/critic (friend of Picasso) G. Apollinaire, as well as the Bard. The word means something iconic and current while also being archaic, with an implication of timelessness. I hope this book imparts the same to the reader, in various ways not excluding irony, as well as an enriched interest in Shakespeare's work and methods which may lend some forbearance of judgment for readers against the strangeness of my book, who can not read it with the "negative capability" of Keats in mind (of which in a letter Keats wrote: "Shakespeare possessed enormously"). Though this book at times resembles curious best seller oddities like Calvin Parker's 2018 book, *Pascagoula- The Closest Encounter: My Story*, about his and Charles Hickson's night fishing trip alien abduction experience in 1973, my efforts are validated by pieces on the current Pirate's Alley, Rosemary James and Joseph DeSalvo produced, Faulkner-Wisdom literary contest finalist and short lists.

To bear the Bard's all-encompassing insight toward Horatio's "wondrous strange!" remark upon the interaction of the men with Hamlet's father's ghost, he has Hamlet say:

And therefore as a stranger give it welcome.

There are more things in heaven and earth, Horatio,

Than are dreamt of in our philosophy. But come,

Here as before, never, so help you mercy,

How strange or odd soe'er I bear myself-

As I perchance hereafter shall think meet

to put an antic disposition on-

That you at such time seeing me never shall,

With arms encumbered thus, or this headshake,

Or by pronouncing of some doubtful phrase

As 'Well, we know' or 'We could an 'if we would',

Or 'If we list to speak', or 'There be an 'if they might',

Or such ambiguous giving out, to note

That you know aught of me- this not to do,

So grace and mercy at your most need help you, swear.

GHOST: (*under the stage*) Swear.

[*They swear*] (1.5.167-182)

During my conversation on copyright for the book with a helpful "tech support" person, Lorraine, at the copyright office, I was told the word "iconcurchaic" should now be placed "in the dictionary" ...certainly, I would feel deeply honored by this and thanked Lorraine while we both chuckled about it.

The artist Lin Emery gave the three book effort a thrilling statement (extracted from here) pertaining to my use of her sublime metaphorical sculpture "Flight" in the composite photographs for the covers of the trilogy *Shakespeare AI* and Vol. 2, *Recycling the Circle*, when emailing after an hour meditation session with the Dali Lama's personal physician: "Your overwhelming poems were a fitting coda... Thank you for including me in your Circles!" What an exquisitely gracious "Zen-engineering artist" she is of the spirit as well as metal!

In 2000 I dreamed her sculpture "Flight" was on the column instead of Lee at Lee Circle in New Orleans. "Flight" once stood in a perfectly proportioned reflecting pool with exquisite lily pads, lotuses and goldfish, to grace the front of the Museum of Art, a favorite New Orleans structure and setting. I regard it as the museum façade's crowning sculpture that has unfortunately been removed to the shadowy realm of the museum's rearward "sculpture garden" like a UFO landing in a manicured swamp. The dream inspired my photographic "odd-yssey" in 2000 in which I attempted to "double expose" her sculpture onto the top of the Lee Circle column with 35mm film in an "auto-everything" Nikon camera. It resulted in the 2016 *Recycling the Circle* cover idea, with a framed print of it presented to Mayor Mitch Landrieu at his 2018 book signing of, *In the Shadow of Statues*, to which he remarked "That's beautiful!" I then mentioned my dream of Lin's sculpture on Lee's column and thought it could then be called Lin Emery Circle. Though he had removed the statue for a more appropriate setting such as a cemetery or museum, he said renaming it was not for him to decide. Lin's deep reflections will remain greatly appreciated as this book enters the wider world with care and hopes that it will help enrich lives of readers with a deeper appreciation of *Shakespeare's Sonnets* dedication on behalf of the Bard's "promised eternity," proclaimed to delighted open minds.

M. D. V. 8/17/2018

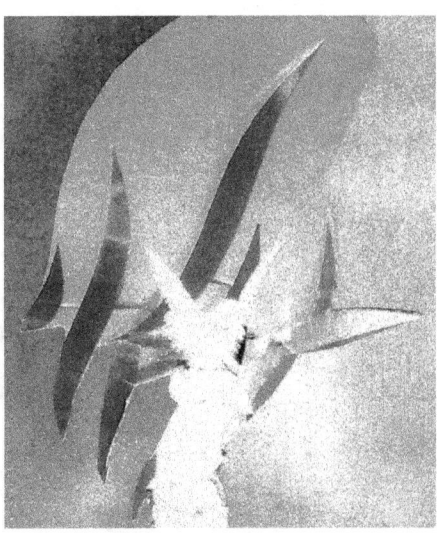

Epithalamic Epilogue & Epitaph

To loving critics who work behind me, beside me or who merely love from distance, themselves as wedded well, but may not know how "good," or those who expect me at the altar of ego or no-go (when what I have is difficult enough to marry without the eternal bridegroom's betrothal), for them this consolation prize. To critics who weigh me in their scales of learned ignorance more blind than the flip side of justice to their own blindness, thin kings of my flittering hybrid's fat stunted imagination, I dedicate to their degrees of "word zymurgy maya" what could have been thoughts of Hamlet to detractors had he survived (as he does here), here's to cool pomposity the parting shot of Sonnet 121:

'Tis better to be vile than vile esteemed,
When not to be receives reproach of being;
And the just pleasure lost, which is so deemed
Not by our feeling, but by others' seeing:
For why should others' false adulterate eyes
Give salutation to my sportive blood?
Or on my frailties why are frailer spies,
Which in their wills count bad what I think good?
No, I am that I am, and they that level
At my abuses reckon up their own:
I may be straight though they themselves be bevel;
By their rank thoughts my deeds must not be shown;
Unless this general evil they maintain,
All men are bad and in their badness reign.

Besides a Psalm (Coverdale's 116: "All men are liars"), this also calls to mind Hamlet's concluding remarks on actor treatment: "better have a bad epitaph than their ill report while you live" (2.2.528-9).
So here is an epitaph now:

My ardent spirits do not desert me for fear
of drinking from the bridal glass, last supper cup,
my book's feast serves both scholar and common reader,
may it serve you well with both hands to follow up.

91

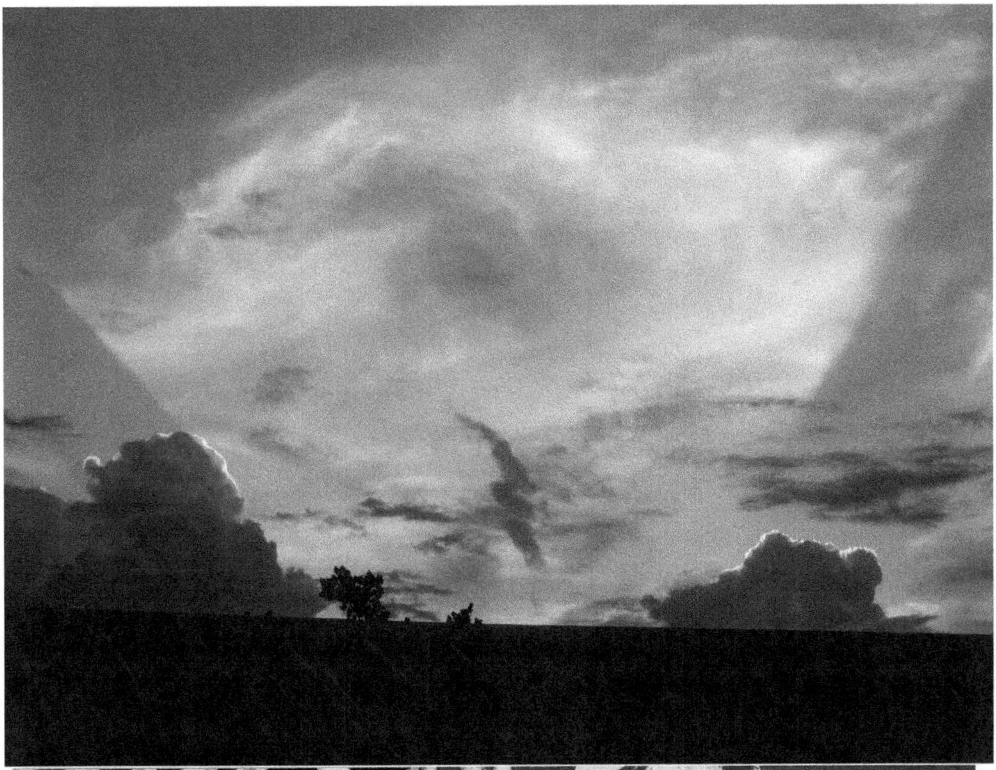
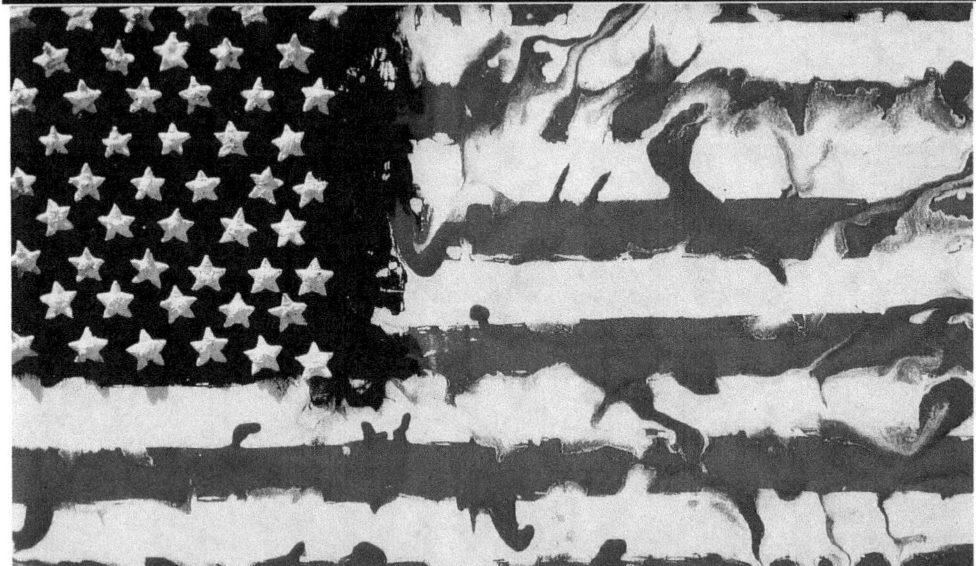

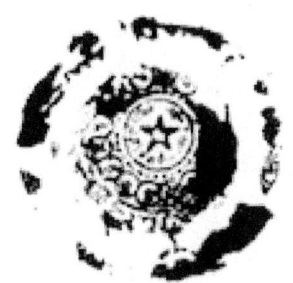

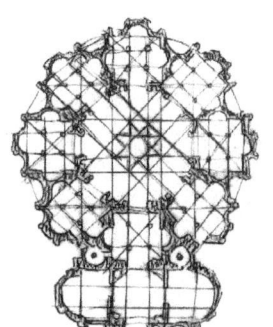

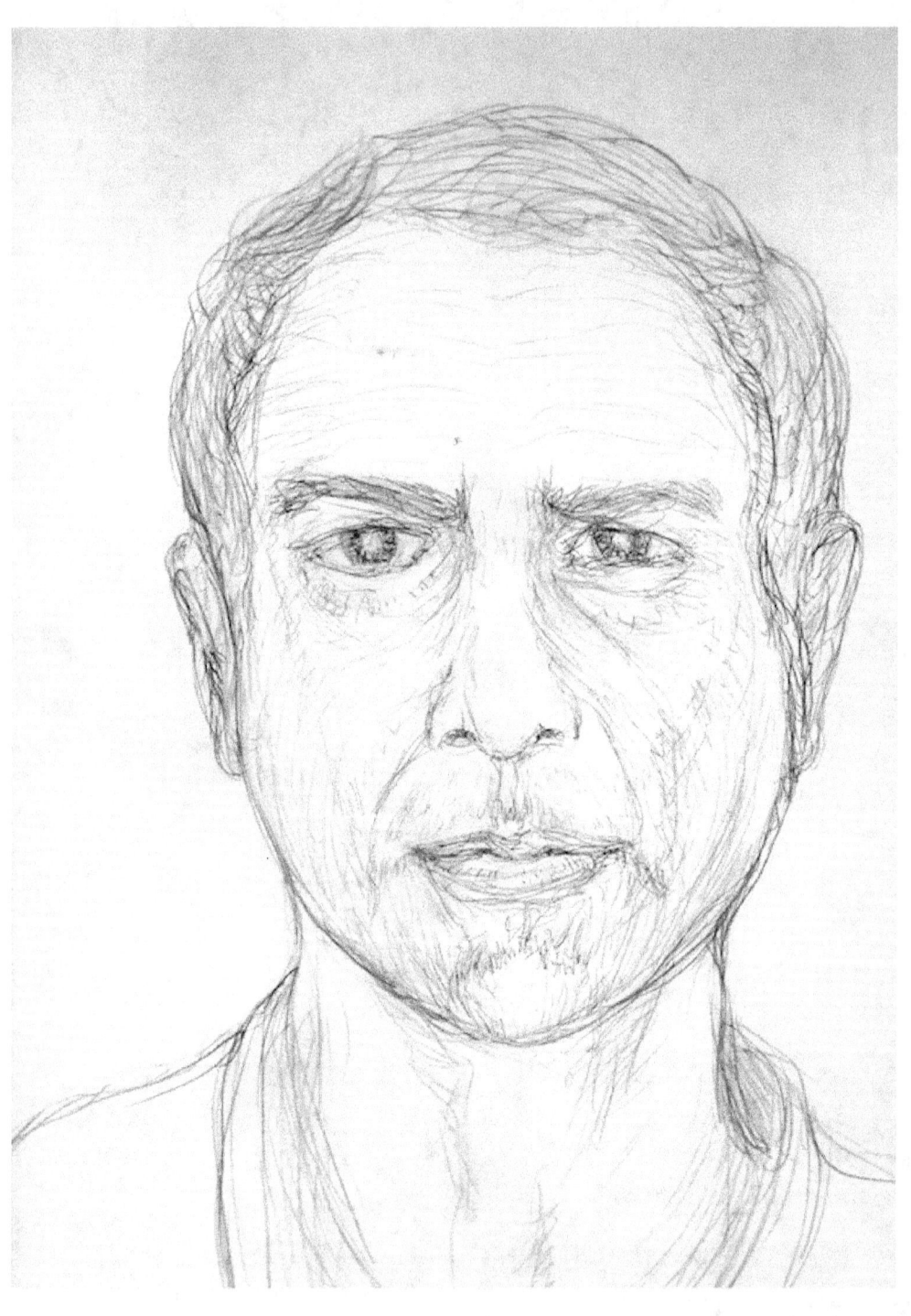

Prints in order:

Catholic Passport Photo
Lin Emery Circle
Orpheus Rising with Lin's *Flight*
Angel Gazes at Spiritual Sun
Night Trolley to the Afterlife with Lin's *Flight*
Angel Reaching from Spirit World
Particle Collision 2
Grasping the Unattainable
Shakespeare's Wake
Hamlet's Seal (1604)
Deluge after Leonardo
The Mayor & Lin Emery Circle (Lin's *Flight*)
Shroud (Space Camera Shot)
Painterly Cloud 1 / Flag
Contrail Cross over Flashing Cemetery Angel with Broken Wing
D. C. Dogwoods, Spring Bloom
Atomic Dali Head for Leonardo's Winged Nike
Winged Nike & New Head
Angelic Double Rainbow & da Vinci Floor Plan
Da Vinci Floor Plan over Stonehenge
Leonardo's Ladies First Picnic, Stonehenge
Mona Muse with Swan Wings
Mir de la Muse
Four Eyed Pointing Muse
Windswept Dirge Muse
Melancholy Psyche Muse
Muse Taming the Wild
Muse Morphing Resurrection
Iconcurchaic Brewer Muse
Romantic Creole Pointing Muse
Leonardo's Leda Muse
Noble Lady Muse
Young Noble Madrigal Muse
Leonardo's Ladies Stonehenge Picnic 2
Petting Emily with the Muse
Portrait of the Muse at Home
Watcher Angel with Many Wings
Orpheus Rising
Susan & M. D.
Radio Wave Clouds Sunset
Portrait of Veritas
Infinity

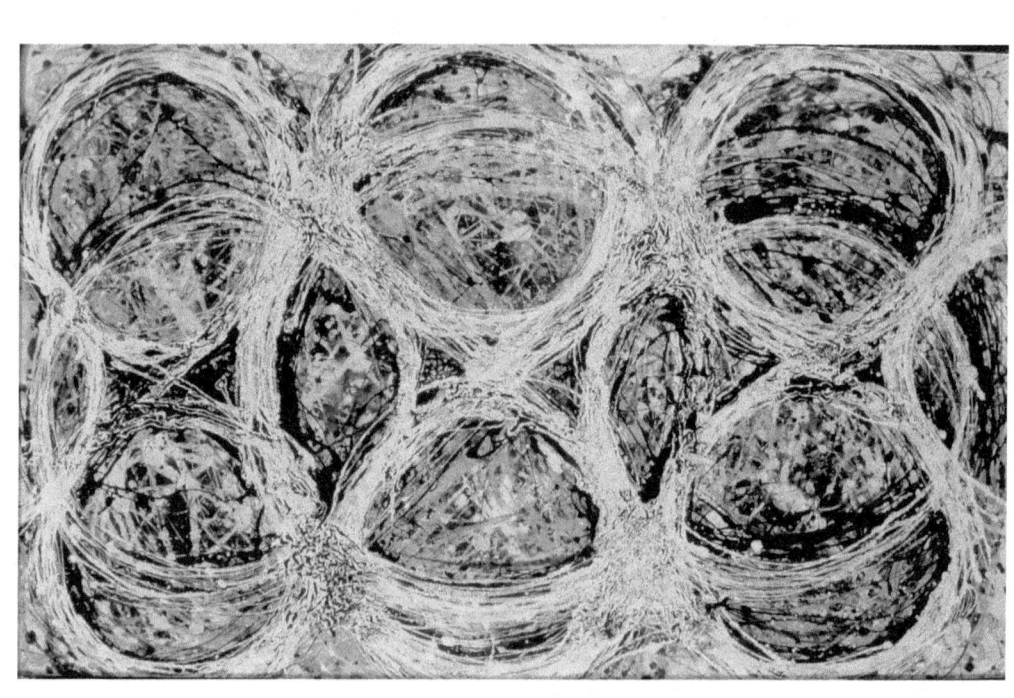